GW00455830

# THE
# BOY
## IN THE
# BARN

---

JAMES
KRAMER

©All rights reserved. This book or any portion thereof may not be reproduced or used in any manner whatsoever without the express written permission of the publisher except for the use of brief quotations in a book review.

Print ISBN: 978-1-54398-275-6

eBook ISBN: 978-1-54398-276-3

# CONTENTS

# PROLOGUE

*To us who know and remember you—*
*Know in my heart*
*I will always cherish you, love you, and miss you.*

This book is dedicated to my little sister, Linda, who still lives in our hearts and memories. She was with us momentarily and now rests in the arms of God.

In Memory of:
Linda Carol Kramer
Born - December 11, 1966
Died - October 11, 1967

This book is also dedicated to my mother, Mary Weil, who was strong enough to pick up her life and move on after a destructive and devastating environment that crippled her mentally, emotionally, and physically. My mother is and will always be a beautiful fun-loving spirit, even though she was humbled by her experiences by the very man who mesmerized her with his good looks and military uniform many years ago.

Most would have trouble comprehending my mother's life is story. These fear instilling events occurred during a time when domestic violence didn't have a name. It was not talked about—lost under the soft whisper in the shadows. The fear I experienced as a boy is all but gone, but the memories remain. Years later, I learned that I experienced not only abuse, but toxic childhood stress and PTSD, which would impact my entire life. The late 1960's was a time of family fun and showing your Sunday best, hiding family problems and anything out of the norm such as drinking, mental illness, and violence. We put on our best for our neighbors, friends, and anyone else who was close. This was a time when things happened behind closed doors for fear of embarrassment or shame. To speak of domestic violence or child abuse was taboo. Marriage was a sacred bond, and divorce and broken homes were frowned upon as something that happened to the lower class or people of ill character. Many people suffered in silence and endured the abuse. Thankfully, society is changing. This book speaks of things that could not and would not be spoken of then. This book is based on my memories, my perceptions, and my feelings. This book is about a family suffering in silence, and about me, quietly living in a world of abuse, chaos, sadness, isolation, and confusion.

*A world of hurt.*

# CHAPTER ONE
## *Early Beginnings*

---

My name is James T. Kramer, and I was born in 1961 in Phoenixville, Pennsylvania. Phoenixville is a small, quaint town approximately twenty-eight miles north-east of Philadelphia along the Schuylkill River. Not shortly after my birth, my mother got pregnant with my sister Shirley, at which time my father up-rooted the family and moved to Ohio in search of work after leaving the Army. My mother gave birth to my younger sister Shirley—a little girl with big bright eyes and an enormous smile. After her birth, my father moved the family from Ohio to live with his mother for a short while. We were a middle-class family living within our means. On the outside, we looked like an all-American, 60's TV family with a pretty mom, handsome father, and beautiful children. However, from the inside—behind closed doors—our life was wrought with what seemed like constant chaos and uprooting: settling and unsettling.

After a short time in civilian life, my father, Terry rejoined the Army. We then moved to Germany where he was stationed. While in Germany, my mother gave birth to my youngest sister Linda. Linda was a darling, delicate, and fragile little girl. She was born on the military base in the Army hospital. Many of the details about those days are vague. I recall only bits and pieces. My mother has helped me understand and put together some of those missing details. Since it was a painful time, I try hard not to pry the details from my mother out of respect for her feelings. When I was old enough and felt the time was right, I talked to my mother about Linda. My sister Shirley, who was only two at the time has minimal recollection.

I think back on the time our family spent in Germany. This trip could have been an amazing, adventuresome, and breathtaking time, especially for my mother, who still lives only fifty miles from her birthplace. She had never traveled, never vacationed, and for a variety of reasons, could never venture out to see the world beyond her birthplace. Her family was a mix of Pennsylvania Dutch and Native American. Her family settled in many of the nearby lands. She grew up in a stable loving home, in simpler times when family was family and home was where the heart was. The fifties and sixties were in their peak, steel was a booming industry, the '55 and '57 Chevy were the coolest cars, and the Betty Crocker cookbook was a must have. Life was good.

My mother was a petite lady, standing 4 feet 6 inches tall. The photographs from her teen years show a happy, beautiful, doll-like little girl. She described herself as a naïve and sheltered girl. When my grandmother became ill, my mother decided to quit school at the tender age of 16 to care for her mother. My mother lived a good life with a large family. Her father worked hard, and prior to her getting ill, my grandmother cooked, cleaned, and took care of the children in small town America. My mother described her family as fairly traditional. Her father worked hard in the construction field and provided for the family.

My mother was only fifteen when she met my father, Terry. A neighborhood girl who was an acquaintance of my mother's went out with him a few times and introduced him to my mother. My father stood six foot two inches with a strong muscular, athletic build. He was six years older than my mother. He towered over her and seemed mature, and although he felt twenty years older in spirit, he was actually only 22 himself. My mother said that people thought my mother and father were the idyllic couple. The age difference raised some eyebrows, but no one thought much of it back then, particularly because he was in the military and seemed like a good provider. Being a good provider was one of the traits people held in high regard. My mother's parents eventually approved of this relationship because my mother was happy and my father came from a good wholesome family. Being in the military gave her family the illusion that he was stable and squared away.

My mother says that when they first were together, he seemed "normal" and didn't behave anything out of the ordinary. However, what does a fifteen-year old with no life experience know? She said his sister, Maureen, and him argued sometimes over stupid things, but nothing that was of concern to my mother. When I look at the pictures of my parents in their early years together, they look odd. My mother radiated a cheery, happy personality and innocence. My father was stone-faced. He had one blue eye and one green eye, was quite tall and rigid, and was rarely seen smiling, which gave him an eerie look. Although quite handsome, when you study the pictures, he appears to be somewhat hardened. Looking at the photos, I can tell there was something much deeper. The photos reflect my mother as a bubbly, funny, and energetic teenager, trying to please and play up to the handsome man in uniform. I picture my father as a tyrant-to-be. This makes me sad.

I have stared at these pictures, sometimes for hours, trying to figure them out. I have tried to determine if you can tell what someone is like by their picture or by their eyes or how they stand or smile. My father's eyes are cold and hollow, almost soul-less. I think to myself, "scary." He had the unusual feature of one blue eye and one green eye, giving him an even eerier appearance. For years, I wondered if I remembered this feature correctly or if I had made it up in my mind as part of the image of a monster. I have wondered what my mother saw in him, but I have not had the courage to ask. My wife asked my mother once, and my mother's response was that he was "charming" at first, but he soon changed to be controlling, mean, and manipulative. Most of his negative traits did not surface until they were married, but there were warning signs.

I found out years later, that my father's sister, Aunt Maureen, knew about his temper and outbursts long before my parent's marriage. She never mentioned these to my mother or gave her any kind of warning. There was animosity felt by my father's family due to the age of my mother, but they never spoke out. I think they thought that my mother would make him happy. Despite years of his aggressive behavior as a child and my grandmother being told to take him to a psychiatrist, nothing happened. My paternal grandfather was in the military and essentially absent from the home, leaving my grandmother to be the disciplinarian for my father. Although he respected his mother, he reportedly had outbursts as a child and later as a teenager. Once, he took my grandmother's china hutch and threw hundreds of Hummel figurines to the floor, breaking each one and shattering the hutch. This was my grandmother's prized collection. As he grew up and entered manhood, he joined the military, like his father.

After a short courtship, my father obtained permission from my mother's parents to marry and they wedded in 1960 when my mother was only sixteen. Why such a short courtship? I think he was preparing to go to Korea. My mother was swept up by his intelligence and charm. He looked like he belonged in the Army, with his straight stance and his chiseled face. He had big plans and sold her on dreams for an idyllic life. One of the constant themes throughout our life was that my father had to have perfection. He always had to have a new car, the nicest toys, and a beautiful home. Anything less would cause great distress. My mother was one of those achievements. She was young, petite, and beautiful—a trophy for him. She was hopeful and positive for a wonderful future. The local newspaper announced their wedding and looked so typical for the times. The brief article stated that my mother was given away by her father and wore a "white gown of lace over satin with a veil of white lace." The article described what each of the bride and grooms' mothers wore.

Almost immediately after my parent's marriage, my father was sent to Korea. My mother stayed with her parents. I was born almost 9 months to the day of their wedding. I was born when my father was in Korea and was about 10 months old when my father returned. Shortly after, they moved to Georgia because he was stationed there. According to my mother, this is when the abuse began. The cheer of the young newlyweds was gone. He started being verbally abusive, putting her down, and criticizing her. This progressed to physical, which my mother did an excellent job covering up.

My father left the service and moved us to Ohio to find work. Shirley was born in 1963. According to my mother, we never stayed anywhere for long. He kept us on the move, and my mother was not allowed to have contact with her family. My mother was busy tending to my sister and I, maintaining the house, and cooking. He was occupied with finding work. He eventually rejoined the Army. Then we moved to Germany for 2 years where Linda was born.

I have a picture of us all together in Germany. One of the few taken there, and one of the only ones remaining. We were standing in front of my father's Volkswagen station wagon. My mother is holding Shirley, and I look like I am trying very hard to smile for the camera. I often stare at this picture too and try very hard to remember. Were we having fun? Was the misery just starting? Was my mother really smiling and happy or was she putting on a front for the camera? If only I could remember. I often try to tap into my feelings and see if the picture triggers any memories. Nothing.

While we were in Germany, my parents had my baby sister Linda. She was born on December 11, 1966 at the Army base. I have very few memories of her as a newborn and very few memories of Germany. My father bought a Volkswagen station wagon there and had it sent back to the US. Occasionally we would go to a park in Ansbach. We lived in the village for a couple months in an apartment. Then we moved onto the base, where we lived in a comfortable apartment. My mother said they very rarely went anywhere except for an occasional drive on Sundays. Our family lived in Germany for nearly 2 years.

We returned to the U.S. when Linda was only a few months old. We moved to Pottstown, Pennsylvania close to where my mother was born. We moved into a two-story row house near town. Our house was a fun place to live for a child. We lived near a McDonald's and across the street from McDonald's was a cemetery. So, there were plenty of things to do and watch. A train ran through what looked like a trench in our back yard. I used to watch it pass by through a chain linked fence that separated from the train-tracks. It was a fairly nice home with a large back yard for us to play in. It was here that we realized who my father truly was. This was ground zero.

# CHAPTER TWO
## *Ground Zero*

---

We moved into a row house in Pottstown. It was a two-story modest dwelling with 3 bedrooms and one bathroom. The house looked like the average 1960's house—comfortable and homey and without today's luxuries. Our family life was best described as ordinary. Everything seemed to be going well and no strong memories stand out. My father was strict but nothing out of the ordinary. However, an evening in October 1967 will forever be seared into my memory. My sister Shirley and I were sitting at the dinner table waiting patiently for dinner to be served. My mother made traditional meals, nothing fancy, but she was an excellent cook. I often wonder where she learned to cook for a family at such a young age. She always prepared a well-balanced meal, which I look on now strangely as "comfort" food. My mother tells me that she learned from her mother.

In my younger years, we all sat at the dining room table for all of our meals. No one started eating before the other. Everyone had to be seated straight under the watchful eye of my father. My mother would cook, serve the food, and then seat herself. We would say a prayer. The completion of this prayer was the cue to passing the food around. Nobody ate anything until we got approval of my father first. In this day and age, this may sound odd, but back then it was custom and practice. The father sat at the head of the table while the wife sat opposite. This is how we ate. Shirley sat across from me.

While Shirley and I sat at the table in the dining room, my mother and father were arguing in the kitchen. I am not sure why they had been squabbling. I remember the feeling in the air, not the words. There was a palpable tension. Their mannerism and body language indicated a major fight was brewing. My father was clearly angry. He was speaking in a controlled manner. I could hear the staccato in his voice. He could be very angry and almost volatile below the surface, but maintain a scary, cool demeanor. He had a way in which the quieter he got, the scarier he became.

My mother continued to bicker. She never took a firm stand. She was always subservient to him. I never saw him hit her and rarely overheard arguments, so this was a bit unusual. He typically lectured and was easily provoked. He was the consummate supervisor. Always monitoring, analyzing, and critiquing what my mother did. She was listening and responding with subtleties. Her eyes were cast down and if she looked up, she looked at him with disdain. She was moving through the kitchen with short quick movements, setting down a pot a little louder than normal. She was not slamming, but maybe not handling things as gently or quietly as she usually did. The tone of their voices was sharp but kept hush so that Shirley and I could not hear.

I looked across the table at Shirley. Even at 3 years old, Shirley was sensing the tension in the air. She looked frightened and anxious. She remained this way throughout the rest of the evening. This tone continued through dinner. I would now describe the feeling as impending doom. Something big was coming. Shirley and I could feel it. There was a crescendo occurring, like a train car gone out of control and none of us could stop it. As young as we both were, Shirley and I can both recall the devastating feeling of the coming storm.

My ten-month old baby sister Linda was upstairs in her crib, crying. My mother was preparing her bottle and getting ready to put her down for the evening as the bickering continued. For some reason, Linda continued to cry. My mother was on her way back upstairs to attend to my baby sister. I got the sense that her crying was somehow interrupting dinner, and this may have been what my father was upset about. My father was irritated and getting progressively more so with every cry. My mother went to the kitchen to get Linda a bottle, and my father had followed her to the kitchen from the dining room table. There were words being exchanged, but I could not hear exactly what was being said. I could tell by the tone that their words were angry. My mother pushed her way past my father, out of the kitchen, and up the stairs to go tend to Linda. My father was quickly on her heels as the bickering continued up the steps.

I was a curious child and trying to figure out what all the hubbub was about. I also was anxious and wanted to see what was happening. I climbed down from my chair and crept up the steps to peak around the corner and watch my parents.

My mother and father were both in the room with Linda. My mother was hovering over the crib. There was a dim light on, and the rest of the house was quiet. Linda was crying. My mother stood at her crib with my father stood behind my mother, looking over her shoulder. Linda's cries suddenly became screams. I could sense my mother's stress, because whatever she was doing was not calming my sister. My mother looked down at the crib and without warning, my father reached around my mother and delivered several strong quick close-fisted punches to my baby sister Linda. He began screaming, "Shut up! Shut up!" as he lost control. The sound of those punches resonated in my ears, and I could hear the change in Linda's crying. She went from a full scream to a whimpering, gasping, and gurgling sound. My mother tried to block him, but he was bigger and taller and overpowered her. I think if my mother could, she would have crawled up into the crib and covered Linda with her body. It was at that very moment that my world changed.

Life stood still for a brief few seconds.

It is strange how a few seconds can forever change the course of a life. How quickly your world can come crashing down. A cry, a whimper, a gasp. Ground Zero. This was the beginning of our descent.

# CHAPTER THREE
## *Violence Continues*

After those few seconds of complete and utter panic, I ran quickly back down the steps and climbed into my chair at the dining room table. I was in complete shock. It is surprising that as age five, I was able to regroup quickly and pretend that I was not a witness to this fatal moment, when my father delivered the life-threatening blows that eventually killed my baby sister Linda. I sat stiff and still, pretending that nothing had changed.

As I sat up straight and pretended as though I had never left my seat, waiting for my parents to come back down the stairs, I looked across the table at Shirley. She also sat erect, stiff, and glazed over. She was in shock. She knew something awful had happened. She was gripped in terror. Shirley sat before me petrified.

From this point forward, events are very hazy and blurry, not just for that night but for months and even years afterwards. After my father struck Linda, my parents returned to the table and ate dinner like nothing happened. Linda was in her crib, moaning. Life went on. There was a sense in the house that something was amiss and out of the ordinary, but everyone maintained a sense of composure. I wonder about my mother. Was she sorry? Why did she not do more to protect Linda? Why did she let my father do that? These thoughts remained with me most of my life. This time period is a bit mystifying. I can barely remember anything and was walking in a daze. Now I realized that I was beginning to suffer Post Traumatic Stress Disorder (PTSD) at age 5. I had witnessed a violent act. At that time, no one discussed PTSD and it certainly was not something my parents would address. They didn't even know that I had seen what my father did.

Three days later, Linda continued her whimpering, sad little cries that seemed to go on for an eternity. The family was on autopilot with my parents pretending like nothing happened, but my mother was worried and scared and extremely hurt inside. I could sense it. She held Linda in a special, protective way, like she was carrying a fragile shell. I don't recall if my father accompanied my mother, but I remember a neighbor encouraging my mother to take Linda for help. One neighbor even made an appointment for Linda with her own physician. Linda was deteriorating and another neighbor took my mother and Linda to the hospital.

When my mother was with Linda at the hospital, Linda became worse rather quickly. My mother was told that Linda's abdominal injuries were too severe, and she could not be saved. Linda died within hours. Someone, most probably my father, concocted a story about Linda getting hurt when my sister Shirley accidentally fell on her while carrying her down the stairs. He had construed various scenarios such as Linda falling off a chair but decided to go with the story about Shirley falling on her. After Linda died, I don't remember a funeral. I don't remember a wake. Nothing was said. My parents went on. No counselling, no therapy, no comforting words, and no explanation. A complete void. I don't know that anyone from the hospital even examined Shirley or asked her what happened. I found out that little, dear Linda was buried in a grave without a headstone, at a cemetery in Montgomery County. Only my parents knew where.

There are lapses in my memory, and some of the details I may have blocked out. The mind has a protective mechanism, and I think mine was working overtime. My parents continued to pretend. One day Linda was there and the next she was gone. Sometimes I have to fight with the concept of believing in her existence at all. I look at her baby pictures and wonder why God would allow this to happen to a helpless infant. I've also asked God why he would make someone as scary as my father.

I began having nightmares of fighting to breathe. In these dreams I was being suffocated by soiled diapers or being drown in water. Many times I wonder if this really happened to me or if it was merely a dream. I have heard that the mind tends to shut down and protect itself after horrific events. It is understood that this is the brain's way of protecting the body and mind. God knows I needed some sort of safety. There was a murderer living in my house.

The fear that prevailed was gripping. No matter what occurred, in the back of my mind was the thought that if my father could do that to a little baby, then he could surely do that to Shirley and me. To live life in continuous fear after witnessing such an atrocity was horrifying. Our family changed drastically after Linda's murder. Yes, I can say that now. I can call it a murder. For years, we simply said that she died. To this day my heart cries for her. I have never been to her grave and only recently found out her burial place. I hope one day I can visit her grave before I die. Even to this day, I still cry when I relive those events and think of my darling baby sister. I know we will meet in heaven one day, which is the only comfort I have.

Back then, no one really knew what Post Traumatic Stress Disorder was. People experienced the symptoms without a name. I replayed the scene of my father pummeling Linda in the abdomen over and over. I began experiencing bouts of panic attacks, feeling nervous for no reason along with difficulty concentrating. I was afraid of my father and studied him in my childish way, watching his every move, and tuning in to even the subtlest of mood changes or alterations in his voice or behavior. I became hyper-vigilant. I suffered with these strange feelings and emotions in silence, not telling a soul. My parents were busy trying to put on a normal outward appearance. My mother suffering in silence.

After Linda's death, my family moved into the upstairs of a farmhouse in Hatfield, only about 20 miles from Pottstown. Hatfield was a small town of nearly 2000 people at that time. I think my parents were trying for a fresh start and wanted something affordable that would allow them to save money to eventually purchase a home. It was here, in this quaint little town in Montgomery County, that life got even stranger and more terrifying.

My parents rented the entire 2nd floor of a cute little farmhouse. My family entered the house through a set of outside stairs and never went into the first floor. Having our own entryway made the house seem very separate and detached. The farmhouse was white with a long driveway and a narrow front porch that the first-floor occupants could sit out on at night should they choose. There were several tall, well established oak trees surrounding the house, and it was tucked back under a canopy, standing alone on a large piece of property. The house was barely visible from the main road. The property was approximately five acres, but as a child, it seemed so much larger. Other houses could be seen far in the distance. I was never quite sure if the first-floor occupants were renters or actually owned the property and were renting out the second floor to us. The family lived quiet and peaceful lives, and we never really saw them or heard them and we certainly didn't speak to them. It was as though they didn't exist in our world.

Right after we moved in, my father began to set up shop. I wasn't quite sure what he was doing, but he had a sudden surge of energy and was very busy fixing up the house, unpacking and getting our belongings in place. Our apartment was a 2-bedroom, one bath, with a small kitchen, a small dining area, and a living room. The floors were wooden, and the walls were stark. There were metal radiator type water heaters in each room that provided heat, and I remember the "ting ting ting" sound they made when they were heating up and water was running through them.

My father bought two military cots for Shirley and I and set them up in the middle of one of the large bedrooms. The room was a big empty rectangle with high ceilings and a couple of bare windows. The room was a clean, blank canvas. However, for a five-year old and a three-year old, living side by side in the center of a room seemed like it was going to be fun, like a huge playground. For a split second, I thought this living situation may have its advantages, but this tiny bit of hopefulness was soon squashed. My father never put any other furniture or belongings in our room. By today's standards, it would be called "minimalism." We simply had the basics without any pleasantries. I honestly wonder where we put our clothes or changed. This may be part of my lapse in memory. I don't remember having a chest of drawers, a dresser, or a closet. At first, we thought it would be fun, but the atmosphere became more like a concentration camp rather than a family home. These feelings would soon become a pattern. Hope would be extinguished, happiness exterminated, and fun and joy destroyed.

Back in those days, my mother and father stayed mostly to themselves. My mother worked around the house, cooking and cleaning when she was not at work. My father had projects around the house. He was quite talented and had numerous hobbies including painting, fishing, and hunting. Their life together had so much potential for being a full, rich life. My father isolated my mother from her family, even though they lived very close.

The property we lived on was green, lush, and tranquil. This was the perfect setting for our family to stabilize, regroup, and move on. The tranquility and peace were short lived. My father's outbursts started out slowly. He gradually became more and more maniacal. He began by overtly displaying his anger, yelling and showing an increased inability to control himself, lashing out instead of speaking softly.

His anger runneth over.

I look back now and wonder if his conscience was haunting him.

My father became more and more controlling. First it was little things like overseeing how we brushed our teeth or ate our food, commenting on small details such as sitting up straight. However, it may have been construed as normal parenting by an onlooker. The intensity of supervision grew. I call it supervising because he watched, critiqued, and directed even the smallest of tasks. He watched everything 24 hours a day, 7 days a week. Supervision then became control as he began hovering over every small activity of daily living, including monitoring our sleep. He would appear at night and stand over us and stare. I could feel his presence, his eyes upon me. Slowly those stares at night turned to physical attacks. Without any indication of an attack, my father would lunge on me, punch me, jump on me, twist my head around and then pick me up by my hair and slam me on the floor. The first time this happened I was so shocked I did not know what to do. I don't know where my mother was, possibly at work. After that, I was afraid to go to sleep. I attuned myself to my surroundings, and I listened intently for his coming. This impacted my ability to fall asleep because I would lay in my bed and wait. If I did fall asleep, I would wake up in a startled manner, listening intently to determine if he was standing in the dark watching me or getting ready to pounce on me from nowhere.

I would wait, on guard for the coming physical, mental, and emotional attacks. When he did pounce, my sister and I would scream but he would cover us up with our pillows to drown out our screams and cries as he punched us and beat on our backs. He would grab us by the hair and shake us like rag-dolls in mid-air, hitting us and throwing us both to the floor. Sometimes he would say that we snored too loudly and kept him awake, as if we deserved being beat for keeping him awake. After his brutal attacks he would strip us of our blankets, mattress, and pillows and make us sleep on the springs of the green military cots. Keeping warm was extremely hard to do in this situation while trying to sleep on top of metal springs. The wires between the springs would dig into our skin. Shirley and I became quite resourceful, and of course we found a way to keep warm and watch over our safety in the event he'd come to check on us. Shirley and I would lay back to back or sit back to back over a floor vent.

While the heat kept us warm, one of us would stay awake, waiting to hear him coming. One night he walked in on us as we cuddled sleeping somberly over the vent. He tossed us around that night and eventually he rammed my head into one of the old-fashioned water heaters. I don't remember much, but I think he knocked me out, and I still have a large scar on my scalp as a reminder. My father was unraveling.

Unfortunately, as children Shirley and I had to endure the tension and anticipation of an attack by my father at any given moment. I suppose in many ways it was like living with an alcoholic, walking on egg shells waiting for the next explosion. I was usually the target of his attacks, although Shirley was a recipient also. I tried many times to protect her when I could, volunteering to take the blame, but sometimes I just could not be there for her. Later it became apparent that my father enjoyed me taking the punishment and thus when Shirley did something wrong, I was the example. One time, Shirley had thrown some paper in the yard. My father got very upset and confronted me, yelling that I was the example and blaming me for allowing Shirley to litter. He was trying to teach me a lesson about littering. The situation could be very petty, but it seemed like anything could be either his trigger or his excuse for lashing out. At first it was the night time attacks and progressed to more discipline and control tactics with beatings as the result of some perceived wrong doing.

The punishments he dealt were initially the usual things that parents do such as sending their children to their rooms or restricting the television. My father got easily out of control in his attempts to control us. As time went on, my father was becoming angrier, lashing out more while he became stranger and quite odd.

# CHAPTER FOUR
## *My Father's House*

---

My father's strange behavior and the noise he generated at night was eventually going to become a problem for him. He most likely realized that our family couldn't live upstairs with a family below and behave the way he had been without being discovered. Even though the house we lived in was quite solid, nothing could block the thumps and bumps and screams of small children. I'm not sure if the neighbors below complained, but it seemed like there was a brief reprieve in the severity of his outbursts while he looked for a new home. My father had to isolate us more.

My father spotted the new house in Salford Station from the road and pulled over into the grass next to the driveway. He left my mother in the car while he ran around, checking the doors, peeking through the windows, and yanking on the barn door. He got back in the car and said, "Mary, I bought this house. We are moving in." My mother had never seen the house before and had no idea this transaction even took place. He had been secretly saving his money unbeknownst to my mother; he purchased the house. According to my mother, my father never let her make any household decisions, big or small. This was nothing unusual for her. She had to adapt to like it whether she truly did or not. So, when I was six and Shirley was four, we moved into our new house.

The house in Salford Station was a classic, rustic 1880's house built on a stone foundation most commonly seen in eastern Pennsylvania. Typically, these houses were expertly crafted and solid with wood floors and extensive trim and a gas fireplace. Ours was not. The kitchen was small and lacked much detail. It was a basic kitchen meant more for a studio apartment than a family of four. The dirty old stove needed to be replaced, and my mother described it as being caked with years of fried food. The metal cabinets and Formica counter tops had seen better days. There were several windows throughout the house and a closed in porch. This let light in so it wasn't as dreary as it could have been. The house sat on ten acres of undeveloped hilly land with trees and foliage and a creek on both sides of the property line. There was also a small barn that sat about seventy-five yards away from the house. Despite the house, the property was an enchanted setting. However, there was so much work that needed done that my mother was disgusted. The inside was filthy. The refrigerator didn't fit in the kitchen and had to be put on the back porch. My mother wasn't sure why he thought about purchasing a four-room house for a family of four. He did what he could on the house, but according to my mother, he wasn't very skilled in house repairs. My mother referred to it as a "dump." It was more like a military outpost. Ironically, the property and many of the surrounding ones were part of a former Boy Scout camp.

Our family was about to have another fresh start. My father made an effort to have activities for the family. We had outings, some of which were enjoyable, others ruined by one of his outbursts. My father was an extremely intelligent man with a penchant for hobbies. He enjoyed hunting and fishing along with canoeing and hiking. He also made his own flies for fishing. He had an outstanding eye for detail and made the flies look real. He also painted tiny designs on plates. He was an outstanding artist; I've seen several of his oil paintings. Many of my talents and abilities and hobbies were the same as his. We had a lot in common, which made it difficult for me as a child to understand how he could dislike me so much. I have learned over the years that his high intelligence was a blessing but also a curse. He had a low level of frustration tolerance and severe irritability.

My father was a military man. He was in the Army and did three separate stints. He was proud of his service, which enabled him to do a variety of things and go many places that he may not have gone otherwise. My father liked to engage me in his military experience and talk about the Army and his work there. When he was on base, he planned a trip for me to join him for a day. I am not sure if this was authorized by his superiors or not, but I felt very special and important being allowed to hang out with my dad on base. There was something intriguing about the military and all the equipment. I felt as though I was being let into a secret club, and this was very exciting for a young boy. I had always thought of growing up and being in the military too. I thought my father would be proud.

My father coordinated a ride in a tank. Although I am not sure he had this approved, I was nonetheless going to have the ride of a lifetime. As he took me on base through the large gate, we got out of our car and headed toward several tanks. I felt very proud walking next to him. He walked so tall in his uniform, and I never felt more important. My father pointed out a huge Army tank and explained to me that we were going for a ride in it. I couldn't believe it. The tank was gigantic, and I always played with toy tanks, imagining how it might be to ride in one. He introduced me to the other soldiers, and they welcomed me and shook my hand. We climbed onto the tank, and I remember one of the solders firing up the diesel engine. Wow, what a sound. The hum and whir of the big engine was amazing as the heavy tracks began to dig into the pavement. I truly felt safe inside that armor plating. My father and his partner explained the working mechanisms of the gun and the periscope and pointed out the other equipment, explaining the important role of the tank in the infantry. They spoke to another tank on the radio. I was so excited I could have burst at the seams.

My father told me to climb the ladder and stand up outside the hatch so I could see. I remember thinking how I had the best seat in the house. I was truly enjoying myself as I got the chance to see my father in a whole different light. This is when the lid, which had not been secured, came crashing down on my little head. I was knocked out cold. This seemed like a common factor, waking up wondering where I was or what had just happened. I don't know if my father got into trouble for this, but it seemed like a heck of a ride up to that point. I honestly don't regret it, as odd as that sounds. I have no recollection of the remainder of that day. My father really did try to do something fun for me.

However, since the outcome was my head injury, my father was angry. My faint recollection is of him being somewhat concerned about my head and then scolding me when we got back home. I was not even sure what I had done wrong. He had a way of making me feel like I had somehow caused this or that. Again, another outing gone wrong. What had seemed like a wonderful father-son experience turned into a catastrophe, and it was all my fault. Afterwards, I heard some hushed discussion between my parents. Needless to say, I never went back to the army base with my father again.

After my father left the military, he worked during the day as a mechanic and truck driver. My mother eventually took a second shift job at a pretzel and potato chip factory. Pennsylvania is known for its pretzels. When we got home from school at 3:30 p.m., my mother would be gone and would not return home until between 11:00 p.m. and midnight. There are times I wonder if she took this job to avoid my father or watching what he was doing to us. Other times, I think she took this job so she or my father could always be there for us when we came home from school. Her heart was still broken after Linda was killed, and she may have needed something to keep her busy. At least this is what I'd like to believe. Honestly my thoughts are that this was her way of avoiding the chaos and punishment. His constant command and control and running the house like a military installation did not create a happy home.

My father put a tremendous amount of pressure on me. I was supposed to be perfect, do no wrong, and know the rules even though they were my father's made up, crazy, and illogical rules. Also, the rules were forever changing. But I always tried to keep up on the latest rule, so I didn't break it. Little did I know that no matter how hard I tried, I could not avoid breaking a rule or stopping his madness. Shirley and I were not allowed to laugh, have fun, or play unless of course it was his doing. There was an unreal and unspoken expectation that since I was the eldest, I was supposed to know better and thus not allow Shirley to do any wrong. My father was programming me to one day do what he was doing to us. I was being taught to control and command others, to set up unrealistic and even unknown, unspoken expectations, only to have others fail and receive punishment. He was training me to be an impatient perfectionist, and I did not realize this until thirty some years after the fact.

I never saw my father strike my mother, and I also never saw him get into a fight with another man. Although my mother said he physically abused her, but not in front of others. I found that in some of her court testimony, she had stated he punched her, choked her, and was generally threatening and intimidating. He had the propensity to pick on his family, mentally torture a tiny woman, and terrify and beat her small children. As a child, I did not realize that he had such serious mental issues intertwined with the domestic and child abuse. He had been paired with a woman who could easily dissociate, zone out, and pretend all was well. My mother could ignore or simply not acknowledge the obvious. This was her defense mechanism. I did not grasp this for most of my life and spent many angry days blaming my mother for not protecting us. It wasn't until I was much older that I realized that my mother was just as terrified of my father as Shirley and me.

My mother never hit us, at least I can't recall her ever doing do. The only way she would hit us was if my father told her to do so. In this case, I trust she was compelled to do as directed or pay some consequence. She was not the hitting type. She typically maintained her calm. I'm sure my father could be just as mean or make the environment just as miserable for my mother as he did for us kids. My mother however never yelled at us, at least not until we became teenagers. My mother could shoot us a glance or direct us with firm words. She was a kind, quiet woman. She was most likely depressed and withdrawn for most of her young life. However, back in the peak of those awful times, we hardly saw her, which is sad in its own right. The more I look back, I think she completely shut down. She was in her own reality and her mind was somehow protecting her from the atrocities around her. For some unknown reason there is a huge void in my memory between the time of Linda's death until my age of six and a half years old. This two-year period is when I became the boy in the barn. After learning more about Post Traumatic Stress Disorder, I now understand that these gaps surrounding events or lapses in time are "normal."

My family continued to adjust to living in our big stone house. My mother did her best to clean and organize what she referred to as "the dump" and rearrange things so the refrigerator was actually in the kitchen. She and my father worked to make this a home rather than a former Boy Scout outpost. Although sometimes I think my father had a hidden desire to run an Army outpost or turn us into preppers long before this was popular as it is today. My father built a chicken coup where there was an old outhouse. He also sectioned out a parcel of land up the hill in the back of the woods. This was to be where my father put up a large military canvas tent and then designated this area as our play area after school. Apparently one of the neighbors had complained about seeing us outside on the front yard until late in the night. The tent was actually really very fun and intriguing for kids, being in the middle of the woods, listening to birds chirping or animals scurrying about. Of course, my father had good reason for his actions and some ulterior motive. It wasn't out of kindness or for us to have a play area. It wasn't to give us space since he only bought a 4-room house. The tent was so that no one could see or hear us in the back woods. This was for his benefit and made it easy for him to come vent his frustrations on us.

Often times, my father had certain rules for our behavior. My father would make us ask "Dear father, kind sir, could you please pass the potatoes?"

He would also make me write thousands of times that we were sorry for something. I recall writing thousands of sentences such as "I am sorry for spilling my water" or "I'm sorry for being loud." Regardless of how petty, there was a punishment of some kind.

After my father constructed the tent, he made a trail from the house to the tent. My sister Shirley and I were only permitted in this designated area known as "the tent." We were not to leave the area or make noise. We were only to go to the house when my father said it was alright, and we dare not wonder. So, for the time being, we were mostly in the tent and not in the house. We would be in the tent at night when my mother got home from work, and she would call for us to come in or we would hear her car and go running. This was my father's alternative to having us out in the yard. We were out of sight of the neighbors and we weren't in the house bothering him. He created an artificial containment area rather than hire a babysitter.

Once my father gave the okay, we were permitted to leave the tent area and enter the house. Rain or shine, wind or snow—we stayed outside. I recall always being cold. The tent was cold. The house was cold. The barn was cold. I tried to justify his reasoning for not being permitted in the house. All these years pondering this, I have come to one conclusion. My father did not like any noise or any kind of mess. He kept us outside like people keep their pets outside. He gave us the bare necessities—food, water, clothing and shelter. The winters got very cold in Pennsylvania with the snow falling many feet deep at times, and we had to trek through this and sit in a tent, do our homework and wait for someone to call us into the house. The hours always seemed like forever, and the cold was unforgiving. To this day, I remember how cold my feet used to get. It was typically on the verge of frostbite.

Inside the house through the kitchen there was a flight of very steep steps that led to the second floor and two bedrooms. There was a gas heater in the front living room that we would stand in front of during the winter months to warm up. On rare occasion we could heat up and watch cartoons. This luxury happened early on in our stay there, but things changed later on. Shirley and I would come down from the tent on the weekends to sit and watch cartoons, or we would watch cartons while we waited to go to school in the mornings. Just under the flight of steps, there was a bathroom. It was tucked in and somewhat hidden. This became my place of solitude and a soothing quiet place to be away from the nightmares and madness. This also changed later on.

Dealing with this monster night after night was wearing on me, and I have no idea how I survived some of those nightly head-twisting-pillow-stuffing-back-beating-rag-doll-shaking-tossed-down-the-step-mishaps, but the fact is that *I did*. This of course was when I was in the house, before he put me into the barn. As his pattern went, his violent behavior towards us progressed. He simply got meaner and meaner as time passed. While in the house, his next pattern of punishment began by making Shirley stay outside in the front yard for hours until my mother got home. The house itself was completely off limits to us.

This was the time he started beating us and he used a broomstick handle that he would go out and purchase, bring home, and cut simply to beat us on our bare bottoms. Later he progressed to trees and homemade heavy sticks because the broom handles were insufficient for the beatings and easily broke. He also began a more systematic way of counting the beatings. Shirley and I had to now count out loud while he beat us with the stick. The count at first was a simple ten count, but as time progressed so did the numbers of lickings. I don't know if he was testing us to see how much we could tolerate, or he was doing this to increase our pain tolerance.

Throughout my whole childhood I could always remember being cold. I never found comfort in being warm even during the summer months. I simply never was relieved of shivering and shaking from being cold. As a child I do not recall the heat ever being a problem to me but the cold itself was torture. It was rare to find the comfort of being warm unless it was in school or at my grandmother's house.

Shirley was a very active, first grader. She talked a lot and was loud at times but that was just Shirley. There was a boy that rode the bus, and he lived the next house up from us. He enjoyed picking on Shirley. I think he enjoyed her reactions because Shirley would get so angry that she'd almost burst. She would become so frustrated, her face would get red, and she'd look like a tomato. The little bully found this entertaining and thought the other kids on the bus would enjoy the show. One day he and his siblings started throwing rocks at Shirley. I knew that if Shirley got hurt, my father would be furious with me. A few weeks earlier I had purchased a little folding pocket knife in a bubblegum machine. They don't give out prizes like that anymore in those machines. The knife was a toy and only about an inch long, but I thought it would be protection and used it to whittle. I put the knife in my pocket just in case something happened. When the boy started antagonizing Shirley, I snapped and started chasing him with my toy knife. I don't quite remember the details other than I needed to protect Shirley or get a beating from my father. Thankfully, I did not actually stab the boy, but the scratches prompted the parents to call the local authorities.

A few days later, officers showed up in an unmarked car as I was walking home from school. They took me away to a hospital for an evaluation. I was there only a few months, but I remember enjoying being there. I could play and eat and do artwork. I played the piano and worked with clay and simply had fun. This was the next best thing to Disneyland. And, above all, I was warm. The staff was kind to me and after a time I actually grew fond of the patients too, even though some seemed a bit unusual. The nurses let me sit with them at the nurse's station. At night, if I had trouble sleeping, they would let me pull up a chair or offer me a snack. The place was quite comfortable and peaceful.

I don't recall talking much about my family. I am sure that I was being observed in some fashion. I find it curious why they never asked me what was happening at home. After all, why would a child attack another child to such an extreme? Why wouldn't they ask if I was being victimized or abused at home? I do not think this was even considered as part of the evaluation, and if it was, they excused it. Then again maybe they did ask me, and I was hush for fear of dying at the hands of my father. Either way I would hope that today a therapist would have addressed this in greater depth and would have at least been suspicious. I left the hospital a few months later and was sad to say goodbye to the patients, the staff, and the stability and safety the facility provided me.

When I returned home, life continued as usual. In the house, my father still woke us in the middle of the night by leaping on us while we slept, beating on us, and covering us up with the pillow. The only change was that instead of throwing us on the floor after he'd picked us up by the hair and shake us, he would throw us down the flight of steps. These stairs were narrow and short but steep. There was a flat landing at the bottom, and our descent was stopped by hitting the wall dead on. Sometimes Shirley and I would be thrown simultaneously and hit the wall at the bottom together.

My father continued to deteriorate. Life was getting worse. He made up his mind to segregate me from the family by creating a space for me in the barn. I would not have the opportunity to help my sister or protect her by taking the blame. She would not see what was happening to me and vice versa. I think he learned from the knife experience that he did not want Shirley and I together as co-conspirators or allies of any sort. We were a perceived threat to him. Divide and conquer.

Developing the barn into a place for me was his next plan, and he started construction of a room within the barn to isolate me and confine me. It would keep me out of the house, and I would not need to come in as often. This would also limit my need to be in the tent. The barn was approximately 75 feet from the house. The design was a mirror image of the stone house and was made in the traditional Eastern Pennsylvania style. In fact, there was a stone in the front of the property with the date of 1881. These were old buildings that had little upkeep.

The barn was approximately 25 feet by 25 feet with a pitched roof. It had a concrete entryway and a floor made of wooden planks. There was a side door and 2 wooden swing doors to enter, and two large trees with branches hanging over the roof. There was electricity and an unused loft upstairs. There were 7 small windows spaced throughout the building. There were no particular smells except for a light musty old smell and a sense of coldness, probably from the stone. A cold cellar was underneath the barn and was accessed by an outside path to the side of the barn.

My father segregated a section in the barn as my room and partitioned it off. Slowly and methodically, he made this for me. The room was set up to the left of the entrance. He used the framing beams to secure a heavy blanket, which was pink on one side and green on the other. He tacked it securely to the support beams and the wall and also created a doorway with the same blanket that could be opened to enter the area. He placed my military cot, a black and white television, and a small floor heater inside to help keep me warm. While living in the barn, my toilet was a cooking pot, kept behind the barn. I had to squat over this and later as it filled, I had to dig a hole and dispose of the waste. I was being forced to live like a soldier. The inside toilet was not an option. During my time in the barn—winter, summer, fall, spring, rain or shine—that pot was my toilet. There was a creek that ran just below the back of the barn where I could wash my hands as there was no running water in the barn. This of course was another one of my reasons for enjoying coming in the house to shower and to use a normal toilet. I always enjoyed the bathrooms at school. I dawdled a lot when I got permission to use the restroom at school and took full advantage of this luxury. I often got counseled from the teachers for taking so long when I had a hall pass. I am a clean freak now, and I lavish the bath, wash my hands religiously, and take great appreciation for the bathroom!

Near our property, there were two houses, just above our home separated by a fence. We were not allowed to go there or associate with the children who lived there. In all the time we lived in Salford Station, I never saw anyone come out of those houses other than to get in their cars. There were woodlands all around the property, and although this was a great place for a kid to enjoy and play, it created a secluded place for my father's abuse. I was about seven years old when he put me in the barn.

Even though I had nothing in this room, the solitude was a blessing knowing he was not present. However, being alone all the time began to strip me of the idea I was even loved. I felt more like a dog than a little boy. The TV had three channels, and they were snowy. So, the TV really had little use, but I still appreciated it. If nothing else I could listen to it. In some strange way, it kept me company. I kept the volume down, so I could listen for my father. It was important to stay on guard at all times. The initial routine was going to the tent after school and then going to the barn the remainder of the evening. This would eventually change as well.

I daydreamed much of the time as a means to escape. I would continuously listen for his footsteps or look out the windows to make sure he was not coming down to the barn. There were no games or books to read. My imagination was always my playground. My parents bought us toys for Christmas, but it was never anything to brag about. I had the big Tonka trucks and toys to push around in the dirt, and I had lots of fun with them. Frankly, they lay outside in the dirt and mud most all the time, as did the little green army soldiers, jeeps, tanks, trucks and other odds and ends. I was not allowed to have them in my room, and I was only permitted to play with them at certain times. The 8 x 10 room he sectioned out became very small very quick. I remember when I was ten years, my father bought me a Schwinn sting ray 3-speed with the big sissy bar on the back. I was not allowed to ride that unless he said it was okay and even then, it was not very often. Regardless, I loved that bike and enjoyed it every second I was allowed to ride.

Today I realize how closely that little room resembled a prison cell. Everything I did was controlled, watched, and supervised along with the heavy critiquing and commentary by my father. Even riding a bike on a beautiful country path was not something that lead to enjoyment. It was wrought with worry. What would happen when I got home? Did I do something wrong? Would my father be in a bad mood? My childhood was not carefree, but constant pathological stress, which now is called toxic childhood stress. Every minute of every day I was constantly worrying, under pressure, or being abused. I did not get any sense of freedom or relaxation until the authorities took my father away years later.

For as evil as my father could be, he also taught me some useful and interesting things. My father loved the outdoors, and thus today I have the same passion. He found peace in fishing, hiking, hunting, and canoeing. He enjoyed tracking animals and taught me a little of his understanding of such. We both went hunting and fishing across some of the most beautiful lands and fields of Montgomery County. We hiked the railroad tracks that ran through Salford Station and would traverse the landscape ending up at various places like the Perkiomen Creek. I recall numerous trips, traipsing through the woods, tracking animals or sightseeing. Even if we were having a wonderful day, I knew my father could snap at any time, and I always knew where he was in the woods, how far away from me he was, and what signals he was giving that may indicate his mood was about to change. I lived in constant fear and anxiety. The fear of an ever-changing world and his every changing mood was traumatizing me. I did not realize until years later that this would take a toll on my mind, my body, and my future relationships. Regardless, I had to stay on guard at all times because his switch flipped just like a light switch.

My father took me canoeing on a regular basis. He taught me the ins and outs, and I would act as a guide, sitting perched on the front of the canoe. It was my job to check for rocks or obstacles and to alert him when rapids were approaching. These trips were often fun and relaxing until something happened. If we hit a rock, for example, my father would find a private area and steer the canoe there. He would then beat me with the oar. Despite the creeks often having houses on the shore, he could spot an isolated area to take revenge or vent his frustrations. I would again blame myself needlessly for ruining what started out as being a wonderful day. Now I know that it was him and not me. My father had a pattern of starting activities on the fun side and later sabotaging them. He was extremely intelligent and talented, but so easily frustrated. He had a short fuse not only to become angry, but he had an inability to tolerate too much happiness or fun.

In some ways, my father had incredible patience. His patience was limited to objects and hobbies, not people. I never quite understood this behavior. He would sit for hours and hours and tie flies for fishing. To him it was a science and an art. He would make a variety of flies of numerous types, shapes, sizes and colors. He paid attention to minute details. He could work for hours on this and never show a bit of anger or frustration. He also painted miniature pictures on tiny plates. The detail required patience and precision as the art was close to microscopic. He would paint these, no problem.

My father was also a hunter. He taught me how to hunt for rabbit, squirrel, pheasant, dove, and deer. He taught me how to track animals. I later learned he would perch himself up in a tree during deer season, and he'd wait for hours patiently for his game. I would often think about this and considered it odd how he could have this amount of patience for hunting, but he had no patience for my sister or me. My father could sit and wait for deer or birds, patiently, always calculating his next move. His preparations for the hunting trip were organized and precise. He made his own bullets, cleaned his guns, and took the greatest amount of care. It was almost emotionless. Obviously, he could function best without human interaction and could manage to muster up so much patience for his hobbies. Any challenges or frustrations would be taken out on my sister and me. Any successes, he would brag about to us.

# CHAPTER FIVE
## *Life as a Child*

When I was nearly eight years old, I was walking around in a fog-like state—similar to the walking dead. After a terror filled night with my father, I would wake up for school, feeling the sense of dread for the day ahead. I realized this cycle was repeating itself. I would go to school only to have some reprieve to return home to another round of my father's temper. School was a respite and a safe haven. I found that I would get depressed toward the end of the day, knowing I was going to return home to him. I never knew what was waiting for me. I also felt this way on Fridays. Unless we had something planned, which he would ultimately ruin, yet I remained hopeful for a good weekend. Many times, it simply turned into two awful days at his hands. If I knew we were going to visit my Grandmother or had a trip planned, I was excited but still had the ultimate feeling of dread, knowing that I would be back in his clutches.

Mornings were not a good time to be around my father. He was always very irritable and even more unpredictable. When he looked at himself each morning in the mirror, I imagined he hated himself for the things he did. I would at least like to hope that he had some sense of remorse or guilt. I tried my best to tiptoe around him in the mornings as I got ready for school. I did my best to get ready despite being completely exhausted and beaten down physically, mentally, and emotionally. I would try to put on a happy face for my sister and my friends, and I would go to school. School was often a blur. I remember many times being present and accounted for, but my mind was not there. I think I had checked out mentally. This is sad because I actually enjoyed school. I think I would have been quite the good student if I attended without the horrific stress at home and with a good night's sleep. The sensation of being a zombie led me to become tired of life. I was stuck and afraid. When I recall these events, I am filled with anger and talking about these times is disturbing and unearths all those old feelings because no child should live in these conditions and under this tremendous pressure.

At this time, my father used me as the "example" for Shirley. He explained that he wanted Shirley to understand the significance of these beatings and to also know that what was happening to me could also happen to her. Once I was moved to the barn, I rarely saw my father beat Shirley, but I knew he did. I sometimes saw the marks on her or her clothes. To this very day I still believe my father targeted me on purpose in order to relieve his every day stress. He *hated* me.

When Shirley and I arrived home from school and went to our designated places we were required to start on our homework and get it out of the way. My father eventually split both Shirley and me up from the tent in the woods because he spied on us one day and saw we were having too much fun together running around and playing, laughing, and giggling. Thus, my father found a new place for me to sit and wait for my mother's return from work. I was to wait in the cold-cellar behind the barn. Shirley however remained in the tent until such time as mom would come home. My father was slowly becoming stranger. He had a new way in which he wanted us to address him when his presence was known or if we asked for something. We were required to say, "Dear Father Kind Sir, May I …" As we grew older, his needs and desires for control increased. Whenever we needed something or wanted something, we had to address him as such, or he would ignore us or go into a rage.

As mentioned, one of my father's favorite punishments was to make us write sentences. At first, he made us write certain sentences hundreds of times and later it became thousands of sentences to occupy our free time. It could be something as simple as "I will come straight home from the bus." Eventually, I developed a huge callus on my finger from writing these thousands and thousands of sentences and I actually think it changed my middle finger forever. I was never quite sure of the purpose other than he wanted to drive a particular point home with us. The punishments were escalating. I was close to giving up. Sometimes, I asked God to just take me out of this crazy, awful world. I am really surprised at how resilient I truly was.

At this point in the beatings, I think the count was around twenty. These had been slowly escalating from harder and harder sticks to more and more lashings. I also had to count each lash out loud for him, as if he wanted my active participation in the process. This was all so sick—my little mind could not even wrap around the "why" of what he was doing. I could only imagine that I deserved this. I thought of ways I could be better to not provoke him. I never did figure it out. Today, years later, I know that he was sick, and no matter what I did would have made him stop. But at the time, I continually tried to figure it out, putting more and more pressure on myself.

Many of these times I'd tend to zone out in my head. I may have counted out loud, but my mind was definitely covering for the suffering my body was enduring. This abuse was stimulating anger inside me, but of course I could not express that anger as the outcome would be devastating. I knew I would have been beaten more and longer, ridiculed more, and made an example in the presence of Shirley. I feared that my acting out would have potentially caused my father to hurt Shirley in some way.

My father always wanted us to excel in school and get good grades. He had some weird belief and would stress that I had to keep my teachers happy. The pressures of keeping the teachers happy at school and keeping him happy at home was simply impossible. Some of this was tied to our handwriting and writing the multitudes of sentences. It was a no-win situation particularly because I was constantly exhausted—mentally and physically. He was unable to see the connection between a proper night's sleep and academic success.

At times the stress was more than I could bear. An example was when my father tried to help me understand the concept of the clock and how to tell time. I was having difficulty in school, and the teacher had contacted my parents concerned about my ability to tell time. My father proudly told her that she need not worry and that he would help me understand how to read a clock in no time at all.

His idea of teaching me how to tell time and to read a clock was to have me stand in front of the kitchen clock that hung over the oven and stare at it. I stood there for hours and hours, and I could not move except to go to the bathroom. I had to stand up straight, maintaining a military-like pose. If I did not stand at attention and my posture became unsatisfactory, he would threaten me with punishment. My father sat not more than five feet from me and watched TV, all the while, monitoring my stance. At random times, he would ask me for the time. When I got the time wrong, five lashes were added to a future beating. For each correct answer I gave, three strikes would be removed from a future beating. He kept a tally.

In the end I was going to get a beating no matter what. This was a no-win situation. Needless to say, I learned to tell time pretty quickly. I did not like this game. Once I learned to tell time, he upped the ante, and he wanted me to learn military time. The entire process started over until I learned military time. He wanted so badly to show the teacher what control he had and what a good parent and teacher he could be.

Despite the weather, my sister and I remained outside day after day, not being allowed to go in the house. Shirley was typically in the tent, and I was in the cold cellar. One night, my father completely lost it and rounded us up, taking us outside in the pouring rain. The temperature was near freezing, the damp cold went straight to the depths of our bones, and Shirley and I were shivering uncontrollably. The rain turned into a torrential downpour. I have never seen my father quite in this state of mind. My mother was at work and my father appeared in his military uniform. He directed Shirley and me onto the road in front of our house. The traffic was minimal; it was very rare to see cars passing by our home. He commanded us to stand at attention and commenced to bark out military orders. The weather outside was dark and dreary, and it was thundering and lightning.

Between the thunder and his barking orders, Shirley and I were extremely confused. We did not understand or grasp the concept of "about face," "forward march," or "right turn." Shirley and I barely gave much thought to what was left or right. This particular night's session lasted for hours. We were marching back and forth and trying to follow orders in the freezing rain. We were extremely frightened, and we both anticipated a beating. Of course, the night culminated in a beating for both of us. We never really grasped what he was trying to teach us with this exercise, but the beating that night was terrible. He kicked us, slapped us, punched us, tossed us around by our hair, and was downright as scary as Satan himself. This night left a long and lasting mental mark on me. I'm sure it did for Shirley as well.

My father had a weird fixation with teaching. He enjoyed it albeit his tactics were cruel and often illogical and unconventional. We never knew the exact objective of the lesson. He took pride in being a better teacher than the teachers at school. He liked showing others what he taught us or what we could do. I often wonder sometimes if this added drama helped stimulate his rather boring life. When I was young, despite what he did to me, I admired him and thought he was larger than life. Some of the admiration for him was because he had been in the military and he seemed so very smart because he was a big engine mechanic and drove rigs and tanks. Looking back on my small, isolated world, he was a god. How sad. This is how most children look at their parents, and I was no different.

The beatings were now occurring more than just a couple times a week. They had become a nightly ritual, and he was spinning out of control. One night, shortly after the marching incident and my move to the barn, my father went outside with his shotgun. While tossing beer cans in the air, he took shots at the cans. Some he hit and some he missed. For getting a marksman award in the Army, he was pretty sloppy, most likely due to the beer he had consumed. A neighbor heard the shots and could tell he was shooting in all directions. They called the police. When the police arrived, they talked him into dropping the gun in order to arrest him. He of course did so, but not before firing a shot over their heads in a defiant sort of way. In today's world, the police would have viewed that as a direct threat to their safety and opened fire on him. It would have been justifiable. But for some unknown reason, possibly because they knew him in our small town as a longstanding military man, they let it go.

Because of his strange behavior that night, the courts sent him to a mental hospital in Norristown. I am not sure if he made odd, irrational statements or mentioned his military service, but his behavior got him into a psychiatric facility instead of the county jail. About six months later, he was released. No one was quite sure how he managed to get out of this situation so easily, but he spent minimal time at the hospital. The time he was in the psychiatric hospital brought peace to all of us. Our family had a sense of calm respite. Sadly, we dreaded his return. We secretly prayed that he would remain there forever. Many of the actual details about our lives while he was gone are a blur. This is not unusual for the trauma we experienced prior to his hospitalization. Oddly, I have very few recollections of my mother during this time period as well. I do not know if we were celebrating, but I remember the feeling of peace. This is another weird hole in my memory. Another blank. Maybe my mind was protecting me again.

Life returned to abnormal when my father returned home. I do not recall us having any sort of welcome home party or celebration. I just felt impending doom. I tried to think positive as though the doctors and nurses cured him and turned him into a better parent or a nicer person. At first, my father appeared calmer and in better health, like he had a wonderful vacation. He was cheerful and looked like he had been eating well and exercising. His skin took on a new glow.

Unfortunately, I was still staying in the barn and my mother had made no effort to rearrange the sleeping arrangements. The barn was mine whether he was there or not. My father's behavior was most likely at its best because he was on probation. He behaved fairly normal, his mood was stable and absent of mood swings. I didn't feel like I was walking on eggshells, but I still dreaded his presence, waiting for the tide to turn.

My father brought us gifts, took us to Dairy Queen, and spent time with the family with minimal conflicts. He was behaving like a real father. However, for me the trust was gone, and my nerves were on edge. Somehow, I felt the storm approaching. As the weeks wore on, his behavior started to change. He became irritable and cranky. He didn't smile as much. The tension resumed in the house. He began controlling every detail of our lives and the operation of the house. Discipline became strict. Shortly after, the beatings resumed, and the cruelty returned. The real Daddy was home. The look of evil was back in his eyes.

At this point in time, Shirley was in the house and I was still kept in the barn. I never thought over what transpired in the house because while he was in the house, I was far enough away from him to have some peace. I used to tell myself "out of sight, out of mind," and I'd pray that he would forget about me. Being away from the flame had an advantage. The distance between the house and the barn also gave me ample time to know he was coming. I would intently listen to the sounds outside, and over time I developed a hypervigilance that I could not shut off. My hearing and vision were hyper-acute. My sense of reading emotions was on high alert, waiting for the next beating or the next attack. I still have issues falling asleep as I tune into my surroundings, listening so hard for fear of being jumped in my sleep. It never seems to go away. My hearing almost gets more powerful at night and sounds are magnified. I am not able to tune them out. I can hear a barking dog, a car door, a bump in the night that others can't hear.

My sister Shirley tells others she was beat in the house and molested by my father. I never saw this behavior in my father. My mother also never saw this behavior in him despite Shirley's claims. My father never did any-thing to me that could be construed as sexual. He never appeared to have a special interest in Shirley other than to discipline her, yell at her, make her write thousands of sentences, and beat her. He was simply mean and nasty and cruel, and he got his pleasure from giving beatings and supervising the most minor details of our lives. Only God, my father, and Shirley know the truth.

Being in the barn gave my father a place to come vent and beat me in private. He could beat me when my mother was home and without her knowing. I think she knew that he beat us, but not to the extent that he tortured us. My father broke several shovel handles over my bare backside. He needed something that would not break down so easy, so of course he came up with an idea. He would direct me to go into the woods, cut down a tree, and obtain a stick. He was very specific in the details of what I had to choose including what the tree had to look like and what dimensions he wanted. I was required to look for a straight branch about an inch thick and a yard in length. This is what he would beat me with. I was beat almost daily with these sticks that I personally cut for him. Once again, I realized that he took pleasure in knowing somehow that I actively participated in the process. Just like the counting, now I was making the beating stick. The beatings were primarily on my backside, but my hands, wrist, and arms would be hit from a natural reflex of trying to protect myself. My lower legs also got hit including the back of my knees. Those strikes were the worst because it made it hard to walk. I have random scars and whip marks on my back, buttocks, and extremities. As I age, they become more promi-nent. The scars on my head are always evident when my hair is short. These are all constant reminders of the trauma.

The count of these beatings continued to climb. I was now being struck at least fifty times during each beating. I had to count each lash all out loud, and if I missed the count or did not say it loud enough, he would require the beating to start all over again. I often wonder how no one could hear me crying out in pain or how no one noticed the changes in my demeanor in school. I wondered many times why my mother did not check up on me to make sure I was okay or ask, "What happened?"

In all of this time, I have a huge hole in my memory regarding my mother. I don't think I saw her very much after he put me in the barn. Maybe I saw her on special occasions and holidays. People around me failed to hear my cry for help. I did not go to her and ask her to help me. Why? I believe I had given up hope of anything ever changing, and this was what life had in store for me. I was often questioning why God let this happen.

Often times, my beatings would result in bruising and lacerations. The bloody drainage would seep into my clothes and dry. Because I was not permitted to shower, except when directed by father, the blood would dry and cause my clothes to stick to my skin. When I was permitted to shower, I had to climb into the hot shower in order to peel off the cauterized skin from my underwear. The water of course always burned so very much. The pain was horrific, but I'd manage to remove my underwear using the water to melt the dried blood from my skin and work my clothing off by shimmying it and peeling it slowly. Many times, wounds would not heal for weeks because he would not allow sufficient time between beatings. In school, I could barely hold a pencil or carry my books. I tried my best to act normal and pretend as though I was not in severe pain. I did not want to draw attention to myself.

I was embarrassed about my family life, and I did not want any of the other children to ask me what was wrong. However, I did want an adult to take notice or pull me aside and ask if I was okay. In my head, there was a voice screaming, "Someone take notice. Someone HELP ME!" Still it seemed that nobody noticed in school or in the neighborhood, and if they did see, then nobody questioned and turned a blind eye. I later saw an old school report that said the principal noticed me limping. So, when I thought no one saw, they actually did. This, in some weird way, was a relief to me—knowing that someone had taken notice back then. But why didn't they ask or investigate? Thankfully now, we have mandatory reporters of child abuse. Back in the 60's, maybe it was usual and customary to look the other way?

Living in the barn, I was an outcast of the family. This has stuck with me throughout my life. I was the boy who lived in the barn, who ate in the barn, who slept in the barn, who played in the barn. Maybe I didn't deserve to live in the house? I rarely ever ate with the family except on special occasions and holidays. My mother was absent or ignored me. My father got into the pattern of placing my food on the front steps, similar to putting out food for your dog, and opening the porch window and hollering for me to come get my meal. I listened intently for his calling because if he had to call me too many times, then he would get angry and come down to talk to me or take my food away. Then I would have to wait an entire day to eat. There were no snacks. No running in the kitchen to grab a bite. No asking Mom or Dad for a peanut butter and jelly sandwich, which would have started a war. You got what you were given and that was it. Any attempts to interact could trigger a beating or being tossed around as he saw fit. My father had a thing about throwing us around like rag dolls. He would grab us by our hair or clothing and just toss us around the room or down the stairs. So, I never asked for anything or made contact for any reason. Once again, my motto was out of sight, out of mind. When I think back on those times, I only entered the house to take a shower and or to eat breakfast before school with my father's permission. What a lonely, miserable life. The barn isolated me, yet protected me.

# CHAPTER 6
## *My Grandmother Eleanor*

---

My grandmother, Eleanor, was my one ray of sunshine and hope. My grandmother loved me. I knew she did. With every part of my heart and soul, I could feel her love. My love for her was mutual. I also felt safe around her. I looked forward to visits with her and was excited days before I would see her. I would count down the days, hours, and minutes. Time flew when I was with her. When it was time to leave her, I was deeply sad. I was scared about what might happen in between our time together. I wished that things were different and that she would take Shirley and I and adopt us. I had faith that she would keep us safe until we were old enough to be on our own. It was a child's wishful thinking. A fantasy in a little kid's mind that gave me a semblance of hope for a better time, a better place, a better life.

My grandmother Eleanor was an elegant, petite woman. She was born in 1910 in Philadelphia. She had the beauty and grace of an old movie star on the silver screen. As a young girl, she had shiny brown hair, sparkling white teeth, a huge smile, and an elegant stance. She was playful like most young children and had a love for the outdoors. My grandmother's father and mother moved the family to a farm when my grandmother was around 6 years old. She was very excited about moving from the city to the country. My great grandmother was also a lovely person and her pictures reveal a special beauty and charm, obviously passed on to my grandmother Eleanor. My grandmother possessed social grace and manners. When I look at their pictures, they look more like movie stars than farmers. Both my great grandmother and grandmother look like they could be in Hollywood. After moving to the farm, my grandmother also was expected to work hard on the farm. She was expected to help inside with housekeeping, working hard to keep the house clean, and she had outside chores, feeding, and cleaning up after the animals.

My grandmother was also very bright. She was of German-Austrian descent. In addition to English, she could read and speak High German. She attended school, sometimes walking several miles or getting a ride on a horse and buggy, but she loved school. In the eighth grade, her parents decided that she stay home and help tend to the farm. This was not uncommon in the early 1900s. So, my grandmother stayed home to work on the farm and help her mother. She lived there until she was 25. I often wonder how she did it. With her sense of adventure, her charm and intelligence, wasn't she bored? Didn't she want to venture beyond? My grandmother filled her days with hard work, riding horses, reading, and corresponding with relatives in Germany. She wrote back and forth as pen pals with relatives, and I have lovely letters that belonged to her. Some day, I would like to have them translated because these letters may give me another peek into her life.

My grandmother Eleanor had a fairly solid start. Her family was somewhat well-to-do, and she came from good "stock," as one may call it. She had a happy family life growing up on beautiful, lush property in Pennsylvania. As a small child, she had a horse and a true love of nature, which carried on into her older years. Even as she grew older, she had a fondness for little ceramic animals, and she kept healthy houseplants with her green thumb. My Grandmother always wore pretty dresses, her hair was always done, and she never left the house without lipstick. Her beauty was inside and out. If there was one word that described her it would be elegant. I often stare at her pictures and try to glean what her life was like. I study the background and look at her belongings. She was sentimental, clean, neat, and proper. She had a sense of order, and not in a bad way.

My grandmother met my grandfather James Oscar Kramer in 1935 when she was 25. No one is quite sure if she eloped or not, but there were letters my Aunt Maureen said mentioned "the ladder." My grandfather J.O., as he was called, was a dedicated military man. He was in World War II and the Korean war. The family moved around a bit, although there were many happy times. After World War II, my grandfather drifted away from the family.

My grandmother was left to raise my father and my Aunt Maureen. My grandmother lived alone most of her life. She left the beautiful big house and moved to Philadelphia. My grandfather rarely returned but supposedly sent checks to help support my grandmother. I did not know many of these details until after her death. My grandfather was quite the ladies' man. My grandfather was married three times. I assume he was suave and debonair, but unable to handle responsibility. I never met him, but I have seen pictures of him in his crisp military uniform, standing with a military posture and a huge smile. One can imagine from the pictures that he was the life of any party and had a huge personality with charisma to match. I have read family documents that describe him as happy and fun-loving, building forts and sled-riding as a child. Many of his older family photos were taken of him standing tall in his uniform. He and my grandmother looked like a perfect couple. Obviously, something went awry with the happy couple in the photos.

My grandmother was a devoted Christian. She read her Bible every night for at least 2 hours. She prayed every morning to start her day and prayed at night. I never heard her talk poorly of anyone and never heard her cuss. She loved other people and did her best in her life's work at the hospital in her later years.

I often wonder if my grandfather had angry or explosive tendencies like my father and decided to simply stay away from the family by being in the military full time. I also stare at his picture in an attempt to try to figure him out. There is one picture of my grandfather and grandmother standing together when they were in their early 30s. They made a beautiful, movie star couple. My grandmother was beaming. He was smiling but I can see his eyes dreaming of other faraway places. It may be just my imagination, but he seemed like a free, wandering spirit, married to a lovely, traditional wife and mother who wanted nothing more than to have him at home. Very sad. Although my grandmother did not speak of him much, she never said anything bad about him either. My father spoke little of him as did my Aunt Maureen. I only heard that when he passed, my grandmother found out he had a long-term relationship with another woman and did not leave my grandmother a penny. My grandmother was extremely heart broken and did approach the military to try to get some of his pension. This of course is hearsay. If so, this is probably the one and only time my grandmother ever truly got angry. She simply did not have it in her. Her nature was to love and make the world a better place.

My grandmother was a loyal, faithful wife. She never took off her wedding ring and never sought out another relationship. She was quite happy living her life the way she saw fit. I wonder if she was lonely without him. If she was, she did not show it. She kept herself busy. For most of my childhood, she lived in a beautiful brick row house in Philadelphia within walking distance of the hospital where she worked. She diligently got up each day and walked to work, kept her house, visited with neighbors, read her bible, went to church, and spent time with my sister and me. She had a couple of friends in the neighborhood. She would stop and chat and occasionally would have one over for tea. When my grandmother served tea, she did so with milk and always with tea cookies. I can still see her lifting her little pinky finger whilst drinking her tea, just as if she went to charm school.

Grandmother Eleanor went out of her way to treat me special. She was a kind and gentle soul. She made me clothes, combed my hair, and generally fussed over me. Special occasions like Thanksgiving or Christmas were spent with my grandmother at her house in Philadelphia. I loved going to her house. She helped me see that there was more to life than being beaten. I would eat like a human at the table with her, and she would talk to me like a child should be talked to. We would laugh and giggle, and she showed me that she loved me. We had normal interactions. She made special meals for me and baked me special cookies. I hovered over her in the kitchen when she was cooking or baking as she engaged me in helping and taught me how to cook. When I visited, I even had the luxury of soaking in her bathtub. Her house was always clean, calm, and beautiful. It was an oasis for me. For some reason, her house always smelled like roses, her favorite flower.

I also have fond memories of her car—a gorgeous 1957 Chevy Belair. It was a two door, two tone, Robin Egg blue with a white hardtop. This was my dream car. Her car had added touches that made it very special. She had the very thick clear seat covering to protect it from wear and tear and spills. I later learned that my aunt Maureen had given this car to my grandmother, and all I could think was what a wonderful gift to have been given. I loved that car so much that I would ask to wash and clean it when I went to my grandmother's house. I even begged her to give me that car when I turned sixteen, which was a long way off, but my grandmother loved me and promised to do so. Unfortunately, when I was about ten years old, a lady pulled out in front of her one day while we were out driving. My grandmother was unable to stop in time and hit the other lady's car. To me the damage was minimal, and I thought for sure she'd have the bumper straightened up. However, the autobody repair person gave her an outlandish estimate, and my grandmother ultimately sold the car to him for a few hundred dollars. To this day I think back on that scandalous move. My grandmother missed her car, and I was sad over a lost opportunity to possibly have it one day. I also try to embrace the idea that it was simply materialistic, but the memories are hard to replace. We had wonderful times in that car—driving to the beach, going for rides, getting ice cream, and more. To me this car symbolized my grandmother's way—classy and elegant.

My grandmother Eleanor went out of her way to have activities for us and to have family outings to spend time with Shirley and me. My grandmother took us to Great Adventure, which was a natural safari-type park with a petting zoo. We had great fun and laughed a lot while enjoying all the animals. During one of our trips, I was in the petting zoo surrounded by billy goats. One of the goats took my jacket and had a large part of it in its mouth trying to eat it. It wanted my jacket and refused to give it up. We were tugging on it, while we giggled and struggled to pull my jacket out of its mouth as it chomped away. Before my grandmother had to go find a park employee, the goat released my jacket from its mouth. My grandmother, Shirley, and I laughed all the way home. My grandmother laughed until tears were pouring down her face. She had a very special laugh. She liked to laugh but for such a calm, lady-like woman, her laugh was loud, unique, and genuine. It was contagious, and I can still hear it today. She would often say, "Jimmy, you make me laugh so much!"

My grandmother enjoyed our company and liked to take us places. She took us to various beaches like Ocean City and we played on the beach. We would walk on the boardwalk and play in the water and sand. My grandmother would also help us build sand castles and let us run wild on the beach to let off steam. The beach was a favorite place, and sometimes I think she encouraged me to soak in the Atlantic so I could heal my mental and physical wounds.

As part of staying overnight for the weekend at grandmother's house, she would do her best to make it fun. Even if we stayed at her house and didn't have a trip, she would make an effort to make it special. My grandmother would make special meals and desserts. She had a recipe for German cookies, called Springerle, that she would bake especially for me. This was a labor-intensive recipe that resulted in hard cookies with a powdery coat and a subtle taste of anise. The cookies would be rolled out and cut and put away for several weeks to harden. My grandmother would place these in tins to store. At a future visit, my grandmother would bring them out, and I would eat many more than I was supposed to eat. My grandmother never said a word, and I think she took pleasure in watching my joy in eating as many of these as possible. She knew how much I appreciated her.

My grandmother was a wonderful cook, and I spent lots of time hunkered down in the kitchen trying to absorb every move. I knew that one day I could duplicate her recipes. This was truly comfort food. I am a good cook and baker, and I attribute this to my grandmother and my mother. Being in the kitchen was comforting. Being in my grandmother's kitchen was a joy and gave me a sense of family. There are quite a few comfort foods like meatloaf, chili, and spaghetti along with a host of soups and stews. She made chicken and dumplings, fresh baked breads, fruit pies, and chocolate cake. The list could go on and on, but the fact was that she would prepare them for Shirley and me when she knew we were coming to visit and made us feel at home. Fortunately, I married a woman who can cook very similar to my grandmother. My wife's mother, also named Eleanor, grew up very much the same as my grandmother. She was also Austrian-German descent. So, there are many shared recipes that bring me comfort, reminding me of my dear Grandmother.

In my youth, I rarely ever saw other family members. Around the age of nine or ten is when I started seeing my grandmother on a more frequent basis in addition to the routine of Christmas or Thanksgiving. I loved to visit my grandmother and loved even more when I got to stay overnight. She always found light at the end of every tunnel, and she would shed that light on me when I'd go to her home. She genuinely loved me, and she would try to show me in every way she could. We had a little routine and she fully engaged me. We would eat our evening dinner, then have snacks and watch Lawrence Welk. I loved to climb in my warm bed and have a good night sleep, where I knew I was safe and wouldn't be awoken by a mad man in the middle of a deep sleep. My grandmother always had clean crisp sheets that smelled like fresh linen. Her pillows were soft and comfy and blankets warm and cozy. I would climb in my bed and sink into the soft mattress. There were no springs sticking out. No scratchy wool Army blankets. So much better than the Army cot in the barn. My grandmother always smiled and was quick to laugh. Her home was my solace. The only peace I ever knew.

When I slept at her house, I slept like a rock. This was so rejuvenating. I woke up in the morning to the smell of her percolating coffee. I could hear the bubbling sounds and would anticipate a delightful breakfast. She knew how much I loved breakfast and would always have a full course meal. I would be so happy. Yet, in the back of my mind, I knew it would end, and I would go back to the barn and the cruelty of my father. Many of the days at my grandmother's house felt like a heavenly dream. I wished and wished, and no matter how hard I prayed to God, I could not stay there forever. After breakfast on Sundays, my grandmother would drive us home. This was a very hard time. Many times, I would daydream about bolting off into the city, never to be found.

I often wonder if my grandmother knew of my father's beatings and cruel behavior. I wonder if she had any inkling or idea of the extent of his madness. I shudder to think she knew and said or did nothing. So, I keep in my heart the idea she simply knew nothing, or she knew very little until the end. She was a very dignified woman, who obviously would have been very ashamed and angered by my father's actions. She loved people and firmly believed in the Golden Rule of treating others as you would want to be treated. She would never have condoned the abuse. After he was finally arrested, I am certain that she lived with the shame that spewed forth and the articles that appeared in the papers. This must have been devastating for her. She did not deserve this hurt, and this saddens me.

When I look back on this situation in its entirety, I know this was my father's doing. His path, his choice. He is the only one that should have been afflicted with the embarrassment and suffering when he eventually got arrested for the murder of my sister Linda and the abuse of Shirley and me, but this crime affects more than just the perpetrator and victims. I have never blamed anyone but my father for the things I endured as a child. I do sometimes wonder where the adults in my immediate world were or why they didn't intervene.

As an adult, I also wonder what my father's childhood was like. What made him like he was? My grandmother was not an abuser and my grandfather remained in the military all his life. You often hear that abuse can be generational or skip a generation. To this day, I am still unsure about what happened to my father as a child. I do know that he was extremely bright and intelligent. I have been told that he had a low frustration tolerance, but I wonder if he had hard feelings about his father being absent. I wonder if my grandfather was abusive during the times he came to visit from the military. I wonder if my grandfather stayed away because he too had a low frustration tolerance and knew it was better for my dad, Aunt Maureen, and grandmother if he stayed away.

I started seeing my grandmother more and more often as I got older and of course the beatings seemed to dwindle for a short time. Although, the beatings still occurred at the same intensity and the count of lashings was always the same, the frequency decreased. I am not sure what happened during this period. Was there a correlation with my grandmother taking care of us more? Did this relieve him of pressure? Was something else going on? Did he cut back on my beatings because he was afraid my grandmother would find out? Then again it may have been my age that was troubling him as I was growing older and getting bigger. Regardless, I always remained on guard around him as he still could flip his switch at any given moment.

Years later, after my father's arrest, I was removed from my family as an adolescent. I saw my grandmother only a few times. I was in and out of foster care and then on the road, traveling the country, and trying to find a place for me in this world. As an adult, I stayed in touch with her more frequently, and she was and always will be my shining star. She was key to my survival.

My grandmother passed away in 2001. My Aunt Maureen, my father's sister, found my address and told me of the bad news. I took it very hard. My aunt sent me a packet of paperwork that Grandma had under her sofa cushion. There were old photos and court room documents, which caused major flashbacks of events that seemed to leap out before me. After finding out about her death and receiving these documents, my mind went blank. I thought I was going mad as all the bad thoughts and memories whirled back into my head.

This packet contained newspaper articles and copies of court testimony. This included original copies of documents and appeals from my father's case, *Commonwealth of Pennsylvania vs Terry D. Kramer*. The court testimony actually confirmed statements made by my father, in black and white, that he hated me. The circumstances surrounding Linda's death were also in the packet as this was part of his trial. He tried to blame her death on Shirley, saying that she fell down the steps with my baby sister. After my father was taken away, so was my whole family. Anyone that I had ever encountered as a boy was gone forever from my life. I had never read the court documents that I held in my hands. There were extremely hurtful things in these documents, which is probably why my grandmother kept them from me. With this packet and knowing it was under her sofa cushions, I know she was aware that my father was cold, mean, and maliciously callous. In the documents, I read his words as he stated; "I hate them kids and they got exactly what they deserved for being retarded." Many of his statements were redacted and blackened out. There were other statements, which I will not add to this book. I have searched the internet and found some of the court documents, which were equally painful.

His blatant response's on how parents should best tend to their children when and if they needed correction was utterly shocking. He believed children were more like dogs, to be abused like he did our springer spaniel dog Snoopy. Snoopy was our poor family dog who never had a chance. My father kept him chained to a stake in the ground. Snoopy's only recourse was to fight or hide in his dog box or run away when he broke free. When he broke free, I would chase him for two or three miles to get him back. Even Snoopy didn't want to be at our house. Snoopy was a sweet, wonderful pet. He was the only thing I could hold, hug, and love without being hurt, and I truly loved him very much. If I would have thought of his freedom, and how he ran when he got free, I would have let him go. He would have been better off. I never knew whatever happened to poor Snoopy

In addition to the hurt, the packet also contained other documents of our family tree and happy memories and pictures of my Grandma with us at the beach. There were pictures of my Grandma and my Aunt Maureen holding me. I was smiling and happy. The good memories also came flooding back. My father could not take these from me.

My grandmother did her best to lend a helping hand if she could, and I rarely pestered her for anything. I kept in touch with her as an adult, but our contact was not frequent because she was in Pennsylvania and I was either in California or Oregon. There was something about knowing that she was there that gave me peace and comfort. Knowing that she had passed not only caused a trigger of my PTSD, but it also created great fear. I have prayed many times over that if I had ever done anything hurtful towards my grandma, that she's found forgiveness for my idiocy, for I love her so very dearly, and I miss her so very much. When she passed away, I was devastated. I know I will see her in heaven, and we will celebrate. I can imagine her welcoming me with open arms, saying, "I love you, Jimmy."

# CHAPTER 7
## *Strange Times with My Father*

---

Eventually, the severity of the beatings increased. Although the frequency had decreased, there was a dramatic increase in force. My father changed it up a bit. So, the lashes were harder and more forceful, but the number was less. In retrospect, I see that he must have become bored and needed variation. I know he forced our pain tolerance to its limits by methodically increasing our threshold and enabling us to withstand more and more. His method was a blend of brainwashing and behavior modification combined with fear and force. This was the perfect combination to traumatize us for life. In retrospect, when I try to process some of my father's behaviors, I have thought he may be a sadist. I have read that the main feature of sadism is a feeling of excitement from administering pain to or humiliating another person. The pain, suffering, or humiliation inflicted onto another is real; it is not imagined and may be either physical or psychological in nature. It may or may not be a consenting partner. I am not talking about sado-masochism or sadism of a sexual nature, but he certainly enjoyed administering the pain. We were his punching bags. His release of every pent-up emotion. He was a man filled with anger and frustration. I often wondered why his behavior continued to escalate. Was he becoming sicker or was he trying to see what he could get away with?

On two occasions, my father beat me one hundred times. These were the most lashings in one session thus far. One of these times, he had to start over because I blacked out. So, the lashings would be restarted from number one until he could go all the way to 100. This strong component of obsessive-compulsiveness was just another facet of his strange behavior. His beatings had to be "perfect" in his eyes. One time I blacked out and when I awoke, he was kicking me and yelling at me to get back up. I had urinated and defecated on myself. This was not anything new. In fact, I had done it many times in the past. Embarrassing and humiliating as it was, he allowed me an opportunity to clean up. Actually, he demanded that I clean up. Cleanliness was very important to him.

After one of these severe beatings, I developed a fever over 105 degrees. I barely remember anything other than that I was extremely ill, but I was so ill my father took me to the hospital. My mother has little recollection other than I was very sick with a high fever of 105 and a kidney infection. She never mentioned the beating that preceded the illness, and in fact, she has little recollection of anything to do with this event. After the beating of 100 lashes, a few days later I have an odd memory of floating down the corridor of a hospital and seeing the lights float above me as I went past on the gurney. There have been many movies that have depicted this scene and mine was no different. Hospital staff quickly pushed my gurney to the emergency room as I stared at white lights above me that seemed to float and dangle from the ceiling. I could hear voices in the distance but not enough to make out the exact words as the nurses and doctors developed a plan of care for me. Eventually I was taken up to the pediatrics unit where everything continued to remain a blur.

I remained in the hospital for a few weeks until I was stable enough to go home. During the discharge process, the nurses talked to me and packed the little things I had. They spoke to my father about what to look for in case I took a turn for the worse. I had such a feeling of dread. I did not want to go home. The nurses and doctors were very good to me, and I asked them repeatedly if I could stay. I physically clung to one of the nurses and said, "I don't want to go home. Can I stay here with you?"

I didn't understand why I couldn't remain at the hospital under their care. I recall one of the nurses looking at me with a curious look, but she never asked why I preferred to stay with them than go home. What a curious thing for a child to ask? Once again, I am puzzled that nobody noticed my fear, and nobody asked why I was so desperate and did not want to go home. Wasn't it odd that a child would prefer to stay with strangers in a strange, scary place than go home? Once again, there was no intervention by the adults. I have no idea how my parents explained my injuries. From my mother's account, I had sustained a severe kidney infection following an injury. I do not know what was said to the doctors or how it was explained. My mother never provided specific details of this illness other than I was so sick that I could have died. I'm sure my parents made up some fake story about how I fell off my bike or rolled down a hill and injured myself.

After discharge, I went home directly to the barn. My father gave me a reprieve from the beatings. After all, it wouldn't look good for him to have another child turn up dead from mysterious circumstances or show up critically injured so soon after I nearly died from a questionable kidney infection. Upon return home, I received no special care and no special attention. I remained in the barn. I got up and got my meals when my dad called me and put my food on the concrete porch steps. I slept with my black and white TV turned on, hypervigilant to the sounds of my father coming. There was no mother bringing me chicken soup or hot tea and crackers. There were no hugs and no "Jimmy, we are so glad you are ok." After a few weeks, the beatings resumed. My father could not stop, despite me nearly dying. I shiver at the thought that I could have been the second child to die at his hands.

*Where was my mother?*

Shifting gears, a bit from the dark side, my father also had a side of him that was talented and bright. This other aspect of his personality was not impulsive, mean, or strange. He possessed talents that I found fascinating and intriguing. He had a creative side with a penchant for drawing and painting, and he excelled at crafts. My mother has a skewed account of any of his talents and rightfully so. Her perceptions and present-day opinions are due to her own experiences of living with him and the misery she endured. He also murdered her baby daughter. So even talking about him is painful. She too has a tremendous degree of post-traumatic stress and has suffered most of her life.

When I talk about my father and try to fill in gaps in my memory or holes in a story, my mother often says my father wasn't good at "fixing things" and that she could not see the beauty in anything he touched. However, I found quite the contrary. My father's personality was complex. In many ways he was a genius and an artist in addition to being a mean, vicious, and cruel person. On a day-to-day basis, he made house repairs, built cabinets and chicken coops, repaired vehicles, and fixed just about anything that had an engine. As for hobbies, his hand-crafted items turned out beautifully with outstanding, life-like detail. His artwork was of professional quality, particularly his oil paintings. He was very patient and could concentrate so intensely on his work. At times, he could focus and tune out the world. His concentration was fierce, and he would create life-like images, and in many instances, his paintings and drawings looked like photographs, just like his fishing flies looked like real creatures.

His talent was beyond the ordinary. One of the paintings he created was that of a World War II Battlefield. The emotion that this painting generated—the sorrow and the detail—was phenomenal. The painting evoked the fortitude and drive of the soldiers, as well as the pain they went through in battle. When viewing the painting, I felt compassion, respect, and sympathy for the soldiers and that their battle was bigger than life. My father could capture a multitude of feelings in one scene. This was the same for his micro paintings on tiny plates. These paintings were beautiful, colorful, happy designs that generated a sense of awe. The beauty and true to nature design he created on a tiny plate were astounding. I had to study the entire plate under a microscope or magnifying glass. Unbelievably, there were no mistakes. The detail was so fine it was as if he painted it on a full canvas. Just as life-like were the flies he tied for fishing. These were anatomically correct creatures, true to form and quite enjoyable and interesting to look at. It was difficult to distinguish real flies, crickets, and beetles from my father's created ones.

Unfortunately, I do not own any of my father's artwork. I would love to have a piece or two of his work to remember his talented side. My father has since passed away. I have a couple of coins that he sent me, but I do not have any of his art work. Having at least one piece would have served to represent the artistic talent we share. I have found that sometimes, I must focus on his good side or a good trait, and I have come to realize that not everyone is 100% bad. People are a mix. Over the years I myself have lost interest in my artistic talent but that is mostly due to the loss of my portfolio. I have been told I have outstanding drawing skills and that I can fix, repair, and build like my father. We actually had many more things in common.

Another interest my father and I shared was metal detecting. As a child, my father took me with him on metal detecting journeys, and we went all over Montgomery County to out of the way places. My father studied the history of the area beforehand and would plot a course. We would go to places that people frequented long ago, such as old granges, fairgrounds, or church yards. My father and I would spend several hours metal detecting, looking for long lost treasures, and most of the time it was just the two of us. Before my father died, he mailed me a couple of coins he collected while metal detecting, and I consider these quite special. It was something we did together, and the fond memories remain. There were very few of these trips that turned bad, which is why I believe I retain the positive memories. He was usually in a good mood and enjoyed walking through the woods or going to historic, out of the way places. These places were usually quiet and stress-free and did not provoke him into an outburst. I still stayed on guard, but they were quiet activities that had a calming nature. I enjoyed these stress-free outings tremendously.

The winter of 1972 was very memorable. There was a massive snowstorm that dumped water, ice and snow and created unusual conditions. The winter snow, ice, sleet, and hail pounded us for a couple days, and in her wake, she left behind a beautiful crystal covered land. Children viewed it as a winter wonderland. My father gave Shirley and I sleds, and it was an awesome winter for us. Occasionally, my father would be thoughtful, and these sleds were perfect for us. We lived in a place where snow covered the rolling hills and provided the perfect place for sledding. Shirley's sled was a round metal disc and mine was a Radio-Flyer with a long wooden blade. I loved this sled as I could ride it quite a distance from the Old Goshenhoppen Church on Old Church Road past the old factory, under the train tunnel, and all the way past the four-way intersection. Near the intersection, there was a General store that included a Post Office and gas station. The scene was like an old Norman Rockwell picture. This was truly a majestic place.

The greatest thing about sledding the winter roads in Salford Station was that vehicles simply did not travel these roads. We could sled all day and go everywhere with ease. We did not need to worry about traffic. There were minimal cars or trucks, and those that might be on the road would look out for children. The people knew that sledding was a priority, particularly if there was a snow day. The town might salt the roads, but most people that knew the area avoided the two mains spots for sledding. We could run our sleds on these hills without fear of oncoming traffic, and the children owned these hills for the time being. In fact, one of the streets had so much ice that it was impassable, making the place more sled-friendly.

Another enjoyable event in town was the train traveling through. The train came through about once a month, and I enjoyed watching it pass. There was a pathway in between the factory and a small hill. There was a little knoll, perfect for watching the train. Every month, I sat on that little hill as the train would go by, no more than ten feet away. I enjoyed the rumble of the large freight cars as the wheels rolled by, and I especially liked the locomotive. I could feel the massive power of the engine and for a moment felt a sense of how big and massive the train was. I studied the cars to see where they were from or if there were people on board, wondering where the train had been and where it was headed. In some odd way, the train made me feel alive and reminded me that there was more in the world than my barn. The train coming through gave me hope that there was a way out and possibly even adventure.

Another one of those amazing moments during this winter of 1972 was when my father demonstrated his creative ability and his ability to be constructive rather than destructive. We had a heavy snowfall followed by rain, sleet, and hail. This weather repeated itself for a couple of days in cycles leaving four feet of white beauty. On the top of the four feet of snow was approximately two inches of ice. The result was a frozen sheet over the snow that you could walk on top of without crashing through. The trees and the branches were covered in thick ice. The effect was amazing. The sun twinkled through the trees, branches and the snow, casting a beautiful surreal light. It was a truly a crystal wonderland. This scenery almost gave me an ethereal feel, as close to what heaven might look like. Sometimes, I used to think that God created these scenes for me to have hope and to know that there was beauty in this world.

I found it interesting to tunnel under the ice where I could hide. My father, however, had another perspective on this. He had an idea. My father was in an unusually good mood. The look on his face led me to believe his wheels were turning. He asked Shirley and me to help him clear out a large area of the yard. We were to create a circle with an approximate diameter of twelve feet. After Shirley and I shoveled, picked, and swept at any snow on top of the ice and cleared the area to his satisfaction, my father retrieved a saw. He began cutting into the top layers of the ice that covered the snow below. My father had commenced to build an igloo. He began creating this as an expert ice cutter would do. He cut blocks made of ice. As he was working, my father tried to explain what he was doing and show us how he was doing this. He liked to instruct, but Shirley and I kept our distance just in case he became moody or angry because he suddenly perceived that we were in his way. Slowly but surely he constructed a building with the shape and form of an igloo. Over the next several days, my father would period-ically go outside and spray the igloo with the hose. Eventually this igloo became clear in color as the ice blocks solidified. This structure was truly amazing and one of the most beautiful sights that I have ever seen. His creativity and ingenuity were incredible. I always wish I had pictures of his igloo. This was one of the most positive experiences we had with my father.

Shirley and I loved the igloo, and we both spent a great deal of time playing inside. Being inside was so much fun and surreal. Inside the igloo was warmer than the cold elements outside. As small children, we were simply amazed by this. Of course, we spent a lot of our time outside, even during the weekends, playing in the igloo for as long as it lasted. Eventually the igloo melted, and we were sad to see it go. However, this is one happy, amazing memory that I will never forget. It was a rare time of enjoyment and fascination that my father created for us and did not destroy.

The igloo had been a short reprieve. Otherwise, I hated being outside all the time. Many times, my father did not want me in the barn or Shirley in the house until 11:00 p.m. or later. Shirley and I would wait for my mother to get home from work. Many times, my toes and fingers were so cold I wanted to cry out in pain. Between the cold or my father beating me, it seems like I was always in some kind of pain.

Despite the rare instances of having fun, my father could change the course of our day instantaneously. This is the reason I was always alert, on guard, awaiting his coming. By being on guard, I remained prepared both mentally and physically for an attack. I was able to position myself in some fashion so as to protect myself should my father be ready to beat me. In retrospect, I am sure I simply looked like a little scared and vulnerable child to him. There was no rhyme or reason for his attacks. One of the memories of "an attack" that repeatedly plays in my head occurred while I ate dinner with Shirley. This was one of the rare times I was allowed in the house and permitted to eat at the table. I am not sure why my father let me in because it was most certainly not out of the goodness of his heart. I can only surmise that allowing me to eat inside provided him the opportunity or an excuse to beat me. It was a set up.

On this otherwise peaceful day, my father was sitting in the living room at the front of the house watching TV in his favorite chair. This was his preferred spot and enabled him to monitor us at all times. He had a full view of all directions. He had the need to know everything that was going on, and he had to assume a position of control. In a strange way, he sat on guard, just like me.

This particular evening, he sat in his chair supervising the dinner he cooked for us. I assume my mother was at work. I was enjoying my rare dinner in the house at the kitchen table. I was being very careful to use good manners and eat quietly enjoying this rare privilege. I wanted to be on my very best behavior. At one point, my father looked over at me as I was eating and said, "You are one ugly looking kid. I think you need a beating for being so ugly!" Immediately, my heart sank, and my gut twisted up inside. I had done nothing to provoke this. I watched him get out of his chair and move towards me. I anticipated what was coming, and there no place to run, hide, or protect myself. His eyes were fixated on me and they showed only hatred for me.

My father reached out and plucked me from my chair by my hair, shaking me like a rag-doll. He was screaming at me, but nothing was coherent to me. I was in a state of shock. My mind was going in slow motion, and I could not, in a logical manner, figure out what I had done. I was on my best behavior. I was using good table manners. I was being quiet. As chunks of my hair fell to the floor and stitches of my clothes ripped and shred, I screamed out in pain. He slammed me to the ground, kicked me and told me to go get the stick. "It's beating time, and you're being beat for being so ugly." These statements hurt me terribly. This incident and his words stayed with me forever. The pain cut so deep that it is hard to even explain. This trauma went to the core of my very being. I often think this is one of the reasons I have difficulty taking compliments today and have such a low self-esteem. As an adult, I am still on guard. I am afraid to let others get close to me to hurt me or to feel my pain. This is not something I ever show. People would never know what's inside me.

Even as an adult, I think back and dwell on this incident. I had tried so hard as a child to figure out what I did and why he didn't love me or why he thought I was ugly and didn't deserve to be treated kindly. Sometimes I hear those words play over and over in my head like a tape recording. I've never believed in the saying "Sticks and stones may break my bones, but names will never hurt me." For it was in those days that his words traumatized me in a forever way and broke my heart.

Day in and day out he degraded me. He enjoyed hurting and humiliating others. His moods could change in an instant. Occasionally there was a rare good day when my father was calm and stable until he flipped his mean switch on. At some point I realized that his behavior was erratic, and there was no predicting one of his outbursts or explosive episodes. No matter how hard I tried to figure out his triggers, I couldn't. In my little child mind, I tried to rationalize his behavior and take responsibility for it. I get sad when I think of the tremendous pressure this put on me. But eventually I gave up trying to figure him out. His words had burned into my mind and soul. He would repeat hurtful things over and over as if he was programming me and brainwashing me to believe these words. Not only was I ugly, but I was never going to be anything, and I was never going to amount to anything. He drilled this into me repeatedly. One of his favorite lines was that I was "so ugly that I could not possibly be his kid." Funny thing about all of this was that he never told me that I was stupid. He made it clear that I was worthless and ugly. One of these lectures was always emphasized with a beating.

As I think back over old memories, I can only recall one time that I deserved a spanking or some kind of non-abusive, normal parental discipline. For the most part, I was a well-behaved child. My behavior never warranted the punishment to the extent or level my father had taken it. The time I deserved discipline was really a foolish, childish incident. I was about 8 or 9 years old and always had a sweet tooth. I loved M&M candies, which I rarely had. One day, I wanted M&Ms in a terrible way. I decided that I would take a twenty-dollar bill out of my mother's purse and go to the store. Out of curiosity, not even knowing how to smoke, I also took a cigarette. The pack only had three cigarettes. I thought my mother would not miss the money nor one cigarette, because in my child mind, I truly had no concept of money or how true smokers always monitor their packs of cigarettes.

I drooled over the thought of how much candy and miscellaneous snacks I could buy with the crisp twenty-dollar bill. I fantasized about sitting down under a shaded tree and enjoying my payload. Somewhere along the way, shortly after taking the money, I got distracted. A few moments later, I was playing outside in the yard and forgot all about the twenty-dollar bill. I was running around in the yard playing and inadvertently dropped the money. As luck would have it, my father found the twenty-dollar bill outside in the grass. I presume my mother asked about it because he immediately came looking for me. I was in the barn when I heard his footsteps in the leaves. As he approached the barn, he flung open the door and said, "You can prepare yourself for a hundred lickings." Immediately, I flashed back to the twenty-dollar bill. It was then that I realized that I must have dropped the bill in the yard, and he had found it. I was terrified and thought for sure he was going to beat me to death. There was no mention of the cigarette, and apparently my mother never mentioned it until later in private.

As I was panicking, I desperately looked around the interior of the barn. The only thing I could think of was "RUN." I found a carry-on type bag on one of the shelves. I began scrambling to toss some of my clothes in the bag while keeping one eye out the window for my father. I then took off out through the barn, ran up the trail into the woods, and bolted through the cornfield. Obviously as a child of eight, I had no knowledge about survival. Little did I realize I had no essentials for survival such as shelter, food, water, or money. I knew I had to run and stay ahead of my father at all costs. I kept running as though the devil was chasing me. For a couple days, I relied on the company of friends I knew from school in Woxall. I did so by simply hanging out with them. I actually got lucky and was invited to stay at their houses for dinner. One night, I found an open garage and stumbled in. I hunkered down in this old garage with a blanket I found to keep warm. I could also change clothes with some of the random items I had brought. I had no plan but was trying to stay hidden and bide my time. In some strange way, I was hoping and praying my father would just forget about me and move on.

Even though nothing in the woods or the barn ever scared me, except my father, walking around Woxall at night was kind of scary as a young boy my age. I continued to return to the same garage to sleep, thinking that I found the perfect place to stay until I figured out what to do next. Of course, I was much too naïve. As I slowly drifted off to sleep around the third night of being gone, I was suddenly awakened by flashlights and loud commanding voices. It was the Pennsylvania State troopers. The officers asked me to explain why I was in this person's garage. They did the routine line of questioning about who I was, where I was from, and what I was doing. I am certain they were wondering why a small boy would run away and be able to be gone for a couple days on his own. At least, I hope they were wondering what was going on or maybe this was another encounter with an adult who turned a blind eye.

Out of fear, I said nothing to the troopers about how my dad was going to beat me for stealing twenty dollars from my mother's purse. I was certainly more afraid of my father's beating than of getting arrested for stealing money from my mother. Obviously, the troopers figured out that I was a runaway and determined who I was and where I lived. Eventually, they took me home and pulled up in front of my house. I was back in panic mode, trembling as they pulled up in front of my house. I was sick. I did not want to go back home and would have stayed in that garage forever if I could. The garage was much safer, and I was away from my father.

One of the state troopers who found me was Officer Rossetti. She was a very warm and kind hearted person. Immediately, I could sense her caring spirit. It was not until many years later that I found out she had suspected some kind of foul play during this incident. She had sensed some wrongdoing with my father, but because I never spoke out, she could not do anything. She had no grounds to pursue any charges of child abuse. The troopers met with my father. I stayed tight lipped, never speaking a word as my father sat not more than three feet away from me at the picnic table in our back yard. It was quite peculiar, but my father did not invite them in the house but chose to talk to them outside. If he would have invited them in, they might have inquired about where my bedroom was, which would have opened up Pandora's Box and led them straight to the barn.

At that particular time, I did not trust anyone, and I had no clue the power a police officer held. If I had, I would have spilled the beans and told Trooper Rossetti everything. I would have told her that I was kept in a barn and being beat routinely, sometimes tortured until I fell unconscious. I wanted to tell her that Shirley and I were in serious danger. I wanted to tell her that my father already killed one child and was working on another. Life was pure hell, but I could not tell. So, there I sat at the table with the troopers and my father, like the cat who swallowed the canary.

After the troopers finished talking to us, they simply got up and walked away. They got in their cars and left me with the madman who simply glared at me from his spot at the picnic table. I could feel the fire from his eyes burning a hole in me the entire time the troopers were at our house. As they drove off down the road, the further away they went, my heart sank just a little bit more. I was terrified. I knew what was in store. My father leaned over, whispered to me in a menacing manner, "You ready for that hundred count whooping you got coming?" I started shaking, trembling from my inner core. The beating I received that night was unbearable. My father was particularly angry and forceful, after all I called attention to him by bringing the police into our lives. As I counted out each of those hundred strikes for him, I tried hard to block the pain and separate the pain from my body. I knew the pain was there, but I was trying desperately not to feel it. I was getting particularly good at dissociating. After the beating, I could hardly walk. I did not deserve this, and to think this started over candy and a twenty-dollar bill. This entire incident snowballed out of control. I still wound up with a severe beating and more trauma.

I can't say how many times I whimpered and cried out quietly in the shower with warm water rolling over my freshly open wounds. I used the warm shower water to peel off the under clothing from my blood clotted scabs that sealed my clothing to my very skin itself. The beating the night I was returned home was not the end of it. My father beat me repeatedly for several days. The beatings overlapped each other into a period that became one big blur. I lost track of how many times I was hit, punched, shaken, and beat again. He did stop the following weekend because he finely beat me unconscious.

My memory is sketchy during this period. I don't remember seeing my mother at all. Where was she? At times I recall waking up on floor covered in blood. Occasionally I was allowed the opportunity to relieve myself outside or in the bucket. However, on occasion, I was incontinent from either the sheer pain of the beating or from losing consciousness. My father demanded that I, of course, get up and clean everything. I do not remember much of this event. I think my mind blocked many of these events for this trauma was so painful, shameful, and degrading. This is one trauma that never goes away. After this series of beatings, my father kept me home from school for a few days. He came up with some excuse for the school like he was keeping me home because I was sick. This of course allowed time for my physical wounds to heal. As usual, I was in the barn and did not have contact with my mother or my sister Shirley.

**My Great Grandmother Teresa Birnstingl Dornbach holding my Grandmother Eleanor when she was a baby in 1910.**

**Major Sgt James O. Kramer my grandpa with his lovely wife and my grandma Eleanor at around 1935. I believe this was just after their marriage.**

**My Grandpa, Major Sergeant James Oscar Kramer around 1940, proudly serving a lifetime military career.**

Eleanor Dornbach Kramer 1941 photo was sent to huband Major Sgt James O.
Kramer during the first part of WWII.

My Father Terry D. Kramer and my Mother Mary A. Arms (Kramer) shortly after their Wedding.

**My father Terry Delmar Kramer leaving for Korea in 1960.**

My mother holding Shirley while I stnd close by.

1965. Germany

My fathers 1964 VW stationwagon along with my Mother holding Shirley
while I stand close by with the sun in my eyes.

*Baby Linda*

**The only known Photo of Linda Kramer**

James - 1965

THIS IS THE BARN I WAS KEPT IN. IT HAS SINCE BEEN COVERED WITH
ALUMINUM SIDING. I'M SURE THE WINDOWS ARE STILL UNDER THIS
TO THE RIGHT AND BEHIND THE BARN/BELOW IS THE COLD CELLAR
BEHIND IS ALSO A LITTLE CREEK

This is me today. Sometimes a little wierd but still trying my best to hang in there and understand who I am and why this happened to us? God's tested me and I strongly believe one must forgive to heal and move on. I still miss my father! I still Love him.

THIS IS MYSELF STANDING IN FRONT OF THE BARN
I AM THE BOY IN THE BARN

# CHAPTER 8

## *On to Better Times*

---

Not all my memories were bad. Like the igloo, my father taught me other useful things. He taught me how to trap animals, particularly muskrat and sell the pelts for extra money. Trapping allowed me some tranquil time to roam the countryside and be away from my father. After my father taught me the basics, I set the traps. I would then get up early in the mornings around 4:00 a.m. and go out into the fields and check all the traps. I enjoyed getting up early and slipping out in the mornings, trampling through several feet of snow in the winter. The smell of the fresh clean, crisp air was refreshing. I even liked the cold light wind that would freeze my cheeks. I found this peaceful and rejuvenating.

I became quite good at trapping. I reminisce about those days because it was a time that provided me a sense of normalcy and calm. I had a brief glimpse of the world as a better place, one filled with beauty and void of the ugliness I had been living. I would go out in the morning with anticipation, hoping that I would find something in my traps. I would get so excited when I found something, and I would turn in the pelts for the money. Earning this small amount of money gave me a small sense of freedom and value. I do not recall actually getting to keep the money I earned, but regardless it was worth it to me. I am sure my father kept the money and that way kept control over what I was doing.

One of the things I enjoyed the most was the small town of Salford Station. The view was always breathtaking. The little town was nestled at the base of a valley with a general store and post office. The population of the town at that time was roughly three hundred or so. I have fond memories of the town itself, as it was small and easy to know and remember local folks by name. Many of the locals were kind and generous.

Despite my living situation, it is amazing that as a child, I tried my best to stay positive. I did this by studying and absorbing even the smallest pleasures. I loved the outdoors and appreciated all that Pennsylvania had to offer. Pennsylvania is quite a lovely state. There were so many qualities I enjoyed as a child, particularly the four distinct seasons. I love the colors of the trees in fall, the look of the icy branches in winter, and the beautiful flowers in spring and summer. Although the heat in the summer was stifling, my relief was to find cool water for swimming. I grew to hate the cold weather because I lived in a barn, but I had so much fun sled riding.

While living in Salford Station, I had the opportunity to get to know many of the local children. Many of us went to the same school or rode the bus together or met while sled riding. We all got along, although some of the kids picked on me for being quiet and shy. They had little knowledge as to why I was shy or a little withdrawn. A little teasing was the norm for children, and it was part of growing up. Compared to what I was going through at home, a few wisecracks from other children in the neighborhood was nothing.

Most of the children went to the local schools: Salford Hills Elementary, Indian Valley Jr. High, and last but not least, was my days in Souderton High, before I transferred to Palisades High in Bucks County. I am not sure if any of these schools even exist today.

Despite all the turmoil in my family, I had some great friends in Salford Station and around the local area. I enjoyed seeing them and their relationships enhanced my awful life. They added something positive and allowed me the opportunity to have fun and laughter in my life. I could actually forget my troubles when we played, and I have fond memories of Salford Station and the Goshenhoppen Church for those reasons.

One of my friends was named Jody. Jody's father was the preacher then, and his family was always kind to me. One of our bus stops was just below the church where the road split. We used to say that the location of our bus stop was meant to keep us segregated from any local kids or prevent us from having fun as we waited for the bus because only Shirley and I got the bus from this particular spot. The first place we started walking to catch the bus was the actual general store. The store, of course, was simply a way for my father to watch over us as we waited for the bus because he could park across the street and watch us. It provided a bird's eye view that gave him ample opportunity to monitor us and determine if Shirley and I were having too much fun with the local kids. He had some kind of built in "fun meter," and if it was too high, he had to do something to ruin it for Shirley and me.

One day during the weekend I rode my bike up to Jody's house to hang out and play for a few hours. Jody and I had been racing our bikes around and doing the usual stunts kids do. We both decided to race down the hill towards my house and see who could get there the fastest. During the race, we suddenly ran into one another, locking the peddles into the spokes of the bike, which resulted in both of us going down. We slid a good twenty feet or so. We didn't think much of it, and we didn't scream or yell, until I stood up. My knee had taken the brunt of the punishment being pinned under both of us and our bikes. This moving mass had slid across the pavement on my bare knee. My shorts did not protect me. I sustained deep scrapes and cuts. The skin around my knee had been completely torn off, and I had severe road rash around my knee and leg. I had several stones and other debris embedded in my flesh, and bright red blood was running down my leg.

When I finally stood up, severe pain overwhelmed me. I began screaming and could not stop. No amount of comforting could console me. Eventually Jody's parents called my father. He picked me up and took me home. My father acted the part of medic, thanking Jody's parents and rushing me home. When we got home, he hurriedly grabbed the iodine, cotton bandages, and tape. He started to clean my knee with the iodine and cotton as he pulled out the stones, wood splinters, and other debris. I continued to scream and cry as he poured the iodine over my wounds. The burn was excruciating and as I cried out, my father gave me that dead eye look, gritted his teeth, and told me to shut up or he'd "give me something to really scream about." He was anything but gentle or comforting. His care was precision-like and emotionless. This was another one of those loving moments my father showed me when I was hurt or sick. I learned something from this about my father. In some strange distorted way, I could count on my father's caring for me, but in a very limited, unemotional way. He could be like a robot. I bit my lip hard as I tried desperately not to cry out as my father finished cleaning out my wounds. Although I whimpered and mumbled here and there, I managed to stop screaming for fear of his wrath. The death look he gave was enough of a warning for me.

Another one of my friends was a little boy named Randy. Although I met him first, I later became best friends with his brother Marlin, whose nickname was Pokey. He preferred being called Pokey. My friendship with both these brothers started over Randy picking on me while riding the school bus. After being slapped in the back of the head for most of the ride home from school, Randy and I faced off on a dirt road that I walked on to get home. We got off the bus, and he was taunting me when I hit him so hard, I nearly knocked him out. Needless to say, it was a short fight. Randy gave up. Shortly afterwards, his older brother approached me as a way of protecting his brother. Their family was quite large, and like most large families that are closely knit, they protected one another. They went by the motto that if you picked on one of them, you are taking on the entire family.

Their family consisted of nine brothers and three sisters. Although many of the town folk frowned on their family as their house was ill-kempt, and they were quite poor, I was not affected by this. I did not care about their socioeconomic status. I simply enjoyed their company and hanging out with Pokey and his family. They were very kind and generous people. They were fun and entertaining to be around. The siblings cared for one another, and they always showed it. I felt like part of their family, and they always made me feel welcome and comfortable. We didn't fight after my initial go around with Pokey and his brother. I became one of the clan. I got along with all of them and in some strange way, I got a sense of what a real family was like.

Another little girl in the neighborhood was MJ. She lived down along the Perkiomen Creek in a shack that looked like it was about to fall into the creek. She was very sweet and cute, and I admired her from a distance. MJ was very quiet and kept to herself on the bus. From time to time, some of the local kids would pick on her because her family was poor. She often wore tattered clothing or smelled bad, and I felt sorry for her. I generally felt sorry for people who were targets because of their looks, how they dressed, or how they lived. I knew what being bullied felt like and could empathize with those being targeted. Even as a child, I had a strong sense of compassion and empathy. At that time, I valued respect even though I was not afforded any at home. I made an extra effort to be kind, courteous, and respectful to MJ. I tried to reach out to her and let her know that not everyone was cruel and unkind.

Friends were another small bit of freedom for me as I got older. It was comforting knowing they actually cared about me, respected me, and showed a liking for me. The pleasure of knowing my friends enjoyed being around me gave me a sense of being free and able to act like a kid. There was freedom to laugh, play, and be happy. Nobody ever knew what was happening at my house, and I always feared telling anyone. If someone asked or mentioned my family or home life, I made short conversation of it and moved on to something else. I was good at changing the subject. I never wanted to ruin my play time and my little slice of happiness. When I saw the movie, "Stand by Me," it reminded me of the walks that my friends and I had hiking from Salford Station down the train tracks to the next town. The camaraderie was the same, and we were killing time enjoying each other's company. Sometimes, we would take our fishing poles down to the creek and fish for carp or catfish. This was fun because the carp were large and gave a good fight. One of my friend's mothers actually liked us to bring her the carp and any catfish because she had a special recipe that she used and boiled the meat off the fish bones to make fish cakes. This was another slice of heaven.

# CHAPTER 9
## *Hobbies*

---

My father had several hobbies that he enjoyed and these were quite diverse. He had such an extremely high IQ that I think he needed as many activities as possible to keep his mind occupied to prevent him from going mad. One of his hobbies was metal detecting. I think he not only enjoyed the thrill of the hunt but he also enjoyed being outdoors. My father and I explored many places with his metal detector and while he ran the machine looking for the find, I was the "digger." Of course, he would supervise how I would dig and issue directives, so I would not miss or damage the item that was setting off the detector. Sometimes he'd allow me to use and actually handle the metal detector, showing me how to operate it. I actually reminisce about those old times, finding mercury dimes, liberty quarters, buffalo nickels, and old wheat pennies. This definitely contributed to my love for collecting coins.

Canoeing was another past time that my father enjoyed. He would take me along on his lengthy trips up or down the Perkiomen Creek. We had some enjoyable times and there were times when it was very exciting and fun to be around him. I must preface that no matter how much fun we might be having, he had his moments when he could switch so fast and turn into an ogre. Not only did we enjoy cruising down this beautiful creek going through small rapids and appreciating the wildlife, I'd be hit with a canoe oar, kicked and half drown over brief moments of rage, which many times were set off over something very petty. He could fly off the handle over my not holding the canoe oar correctly, not stroking the water correctly, or not looking out for rocks or debris. He would suddenly go into a rage and throw me into the water. In fact, when I was quite young, this is how I learned to swim. It gives the old adage to the term "sink or swim." It was an aluminum canoe and actually one of the best. No matter what the circumstances, he would belittle or find something to pick on me over, which in turn would ruin the whole trip.

One of the best things I enjoyed doing with him was fishing. My father was an avid fisherman who enjoyed the sport to its fullest. We primarily fished for trout, and he taught me many of his handy tricks in landing them. He also taught me to tie my own hooks and knots. Fathers throughout history taught their sons how to fish. So, my father felt he was fulfilling his responsibility. It is ironic, as I try many times to think of my father in a brighter light, saying "My father took me fishing and taught me how to fish."

The strangest experience is that my father could be talking to me, smiling and laughing, being excited over me catching a fish and then he would suddenly snap. I could see it in his eyes. It was as if his pupils would dilate and this terrible, hateful look would take hold. His eyes would become dark and cold and an evil expression would overtake his face. His entire demeanor would change, and he took on another look about himself, almost like a completely different personality. My heart would always sink, and I would know it was going to get ugly and scary for me. I've spent many days thinking over his attitude changes and what triggered his madness. To this day I have no clue. At times, I think he had a multiple personality disorder or some kind of mental illness, but why the sudden switches?

My father also enjoyed and loved hunting. He would sometimes take me along, but I was only allowed to watch and learn. He took me up in the cornfield above our house in Salford Station. He let me shoot the twelve-gauge double barrel shotgun. He also bought me an old Daisy Pump Action BB Gun, which I would run around with in the woods shooting at tin cans and such. I had no idea why my father allowed me to do this on my own, but he also stalked me through the woods. One day, he caught me shooting at cows in the butt. He, in turn, corrected me with a stern beating, kicking me around, slapping me, and later beating me with the stick in the barn.

Shortly after that, he made me take a hunter and gun safety course. I learned this was a requirement for getting a hunting license in the state of Pennsylvania. I enjoyed this class and passed it with flying colors and got my license. My father loved to hunt, always for the purpose of food for the table. He was a crack shot, and it never failed there was venison, turkey, duck, quail, squirrel, rabbit, dove, or pheasant that he shot and brought home. He taught me well. He also was allowed to use a target range near the church, and he would take me with him to help zero in his scope. He had a scope on his gun, and I would love to watch him shoot. He also had a separately mounted scope that sat on a tripod and enabled me to watch him shoot his target and tell him where he hit on the target. As an adult, I am an avid lover of guns and am fairly good because of his teachings. I learned later in my years that he was a marksman in the military and given a medal. This would explain why he shot with expertise.

There was always the impression that hunting, fishing, and hiking were ways for my father and I to connect. I think it was his way of trying to bond. I was so excited to get my hunting license and to be able to hunt with my father in the following years to come. I felt as though my father was giving me some responsibility and respect. Despite the beatings continuing, there was a little less of them as I was growing older. I was also getting bigger, and I think my father was thinking to himself about me and worried for his own safety. In addition, hunting with him was a risky adventure.

My father had planned out our hunting trips like a military deployment. He planned out the trip in advance and prepared the equipment the night before. We would get up very early, long before the sun would rise. I recall one trip in particular. At four in the morning, we prepared to go turkey hunting. As I ate my cereal, my father loaded up the car. I was very excited that I was heading off with my dad to hunt, something only grown-ups could do. It was the first time I was officially going to use my newly acquired hunting license. He also bought me my own shotgun, and I was going to get to use it for the first time. I was so amped to go hunting, and it was in the back of my mind that this was my opportunity for my dad to see what I could do and maybe make him happy. I always my wished that this would give him a reason to stop beating me. Maybe I could do something just right.

My father's double barreled twelve-gauge shotgun was a very powerful gun. When I shot it, the recoil knocked me down and threw me back a distance. The first time I shot it, I hit a coffee can I was aiming at from about thirty feet. I never found the can itself, but I do recall finding myself lying on the ground about five feet back from where I was standing. I remember staring at the sky thinking I was dead. Then of course I could feel the heavy weight of the shotgun in my hands and realizing the force of the gun had knocked me off my feet. My father was amused and was actually laughing out loud. He laughed so hard he had tears. He is the one that talked me into pulling both barrels, not thinking I would actually do it. Needless to say, I found fondness and respect for guns, and I'd ask to shoot as often as I could after that day.

Because our house was located in the back country, we could shoot right out in the back yard. Back then it was not considered city limits. The only thing that was behind our targets was a hill that rose about fifty yards to a cornfield. At the same time, it gave us the distance to sight in our guns or simply shoot the shotgun. These were all great times.

# CHAPTER 10

## *Holidays*

---

My father loved Christmas. He seemed unusually chipper and in high spirits for the majority of the season. He liked the music, as do I, and he would often watch Christmas shows on TV. He would decorate the house, and at times, he would allow me to come into the house to just to sit and watch TV and be part of the family for some unknown reason. We had a fully decorated Christmas tree—lights, ornaments, and lots of varieties of cookies.

My father always had a way of ruining the holiest of seasons. A memorable moment was one Christmas when Shirley and I visited Grandma Eleanor. We had gotten up early, dressed in our Sunday best, and gone to church with my father and mother and then attended dinner at Grandma's. Her house was always warm and welcoming, with plenty of decorations and my favorite cookies. Her house was always peaceful and warm and particularly so on Christmas. It was almost like something you'd see on a warm and fuzzy Christmas special on television. We always enjoyed our grandmother's house, her wonderful cooking, her beautiful table settings, and the holiday atmosphere. Her Christmas tree was perfectly decorated, and she always had white lights each year, which she said represented purity. She celebrated Christmas for its true meaning, the birth of Christ.

My grandmother went out of her way to make Christmas special for Shirley and me. I have extremely fond memories of my grandmother, and I loved her so very dearly. I truly miss her and think of her almost every day. One of those special memories was the sweet smell of her home and all the wonderful little treats she would make especially for us. There was one cookie she would make especially for me.

Over the years of learning to fend for myself, I have learned to cook very well. I have attempted to make these cookies on several occasions, and I have my grandmother's recipe. It is hard to get the recipe correct. The first time I made them, I could have built a brick house out of them, because they were so hard. The taste of course was there but the texture was not. Those people who were kind enough to eat them liked them, only to complain of their hardness. However, after several years of making these cookies and having the help of my aunt Maureen giving me my grandma's original recipe, I finally got them down to a science. With each nibble of cookie, I am flooded with the warm pleasant memories of my Grandma, her beautiful home, and the warm, loving, welcoming environment she created for both Shirley and me.

On one occasion, my family was at my grandma's house and having a wonderful time. Our family sat like we did each year in front of the tree opening the gifts Grandma would give us. Among the many gifts, Grandma bought Shirley a four-foot teddy bear to hug and hold to comfort her when she needed. The bear was big and soft and furry and almost taller than Shirley. Shirley was thrilled of course and squeezed and hugged that bear like it was a life-line for her. Grandma had bought me my very first guitar. I was ecstatic because I had always loved music and thought this was my chance to play one of my favorite instruments. This would help entertain me while I was locked away in the barn by myself. I daydreamed about strumming away on my guitar, relaxing, and learning music. At the time, my father seemed just as excited for both Shirley and I as we opened these gifts. My grandma had really impressed us this year.

As we drove home, I continued to daydream about playing my guitar as we pulled up to the house. My father was smiling and acting as if nothing was wrong. He asked us to show him our presents again from Grandma, which we happily did. He then asked us to follow him, as we went outside the front door and down through the yard. Shirley and I were puzzled by his actions and could only assume he was going to take a picture with us and our new toys. We could not be so lucky. He made us place our toys on the trash pile, while he tossed gasoline on them and threw a match to it. I was absolutely stunned, as was Shirley. We stood there and sobbed as he burned our Christmas gifts that year. He left us looking at the fire and walked away. Once again, I have no idea where my mother was because she was with us when we arrived home.

Shirley and I didn't have many toys, and of course we had no idea why on earth he was so bothered by these gifts. There was no rational explanation for his actions or why he would want to be so hurtful towards Shirley and me or disrespectful to his mother. Nothing was said, and he remained completely calm over his actions. I remember looking over at Shirley, who was also sobbing, and I had no words to comfort her as my heart was equally broken.

The sound of crying or sobbing triggers me and often reminds me of those horrible days of my childhood. I think of standing in front of this fire watching our toys burn and trying desperately to hush my cries when I really wanted to scream. It's funny when I think about how I am affected today with sounds around me and have a hard time with children screaming. To think of a child screaming for no apparent reason thwarts off the idea the child might be hurt or may be even in grave danger. This thought may stem back to my youthful days when my father caught us running around in the woods, playing and screaming very loudly. He explained then the only reason children should scream like that is if they are in danger or hurt. To this day I find myself sensitive to the screams of children.

On other holidays, we also went to my Grandmother's house. Typically, the visit went well. We all sat at the dinner table. My father made it a point that both Shirley and I use good table manners. We had to ask for everything on the table and never reach. If we reached for anything on the table without asking, it was cause for a beating, which we were sure to have when we got home. My grandmother had no idea of this, and one evening at her house during a holiday dinner, she was puzzled by our actions, and the way we asked for things at the table. I could tell by her expression and her raised eyebrow. She would look at us oddly when we would say things such as, "Dear father kind sir, may I have the potatoes" or whatever it might be. This action went on for a year or more. This was some outward evidence of his unraveling.

Once, we were visiting my Grandma for another holiday, when my father knocked me off my chair while at the dinner table in front of my grandmother. He backhanded me and I flew across the room. I think it was because I did not use the proper format for requesting the food item I wanted. My Grandma immediately got angry with him. There was of course some adult-like conversation and she made us leave her house. She demanded that he leave immediately. My father never touched either one of us in front of her again.

We did not celebrate birthdays. I vaguely recall an occasional cake but there was no celebrating in our house. My grandmother would make us a cake and have gifts when we visited her around our birthdays, but typically birthdays were like any other day. I figured that my father did not really want us; therefore, our birth was not cause for celebration. As odd as it may seem, my father would occasionally appear with a gift. He could be so unpredictable, so moody. The only thing that was predictable was his violence. I learned to live in a constant state of chaos and violence. So, the joy and celebration that other children may have experienced, my world was void of those. I didn't know what a family get together, a holiday, or a party truly was. I learned to dread any type of special occasion because they turned out bad.

# CHAPTER 11
## *Shirley*

My younger sister Shirley was a funny girl. My life as a child would have been quite lonely without her. We lived with a mantra of "all for one and one for all" for many years after Linda's death, until we became teenagers. We had a bond that no one could break. Not child welfare, foster homes, or my father.

Shirley was a petite and skinny little kid. She had the biggest smile with large perfect teeth. She had an ornery look about her as if she was thinking about her next adventure or how she was going to get into something she shouldn't. Shirley was very cute with her strawberry blond hair and freckles. She was younger and shorter than me but could be louder and way more stubborn.

I have fond memories of her up until late adulthood. Various circumstances caused us to part ways, particularly when my father passed away,

As a child, Shirley could get into trouble without trying, and as her keeper as set forth by my father, I would run after her and make sure she didn't make a mess or do anything wrong. Regardless of what I did, Shirley could get herself into a pickle. We did laugh a lot despite our pain and suffering. When we would go for walks, she would get muddy or fall in a creek. She would get into squabbles on the bus or at school. She would also go to school without sleep because my father would beat her and wake her up too. She would be dozing off in class. Despite all of this, we would try to giggle and laugh.

Playing in the snow and with our sleds was always fun. However, Shirley would get us side-tracked and get us into some kind of incident. There were numerous occasions when she would fly down the hill on her round metal disk sled, go over a hill, and wind up soaking wet in a creek. We would laugh and laugh as we ran home to get her dried off and changed before she got in trouble. Shirley would be the kid that fell in the mud puddle or stepped on a rock and fell in the water. Then of course we would panic but also laugh until we cried. There were many good times, and I don't know what I would have done without her or she without me.

Much like myself, Shirley viewed school as a break from our awful home life. We would be excited for the break for Christmas. We also knew that our father liked Christmas and despite him ruining many of them, he would be in a good mood more often through the months of November through January. After the holiday season, we looked forward to Spring and the warmer weather. One Spring, after coming home from school, Shirley and I went to our designated places and completed our homework. I snuck up to the tent to hang out with Shirley, thinking my father would never know. Of course, we grew fond of the idea that our father had no idea that we were getting together after our homework and playing in the woods. This went on for several weeks. I got so tired of sitting in the cold room, getting out and running around in the sun was a relief. We gradually got braver and decided we were going to sneak into the house to make sandwiches or grab snacks. Shirley and I both climbed through the bathroom window. My father must have sensed something or felt something was out of place. As I previously mentioned, he too was hypervigilant. As we snuck into the house, my father was hiding upstairs, and he came down the steps, only to confront us and ask us what we were doing. The beating was horrible that day for both of us, and we never did get those snacks.

Shirley and I found trouble one way or the other. When we got in trouble, we really got in trouble. Before taking my gun class or becoming a licensed hunter, I often played with a BB gun. However, being child minded, I liked to play with a 22-caliber long rifle that my father left in the barn. I'm not sure why he left it there, but I was thinking this gun had no more power than my BB gun, and thus pointed it at the barn door knowing my sister was inside. My intention was to scare her, and I thought it would be funny. I imagined her shrieking and running around screaming then breaking into sheer laughter. However, this turned out quite different. I pointed the rifle low on the floor, and it was a good thing. I had no clue the bullet would go through the door. Of course, as luck would have it, the bullet penetrated the door and went through the door and right through my sister Shirley's shin.

When I heard her scream, I panicked and became utterly frightened. Shirley had slung open the garage door and bolted. She was running as if she was running for her life. I never imagined the bullet would travel through that door. I sincerely thought it would "ping" off the door. The whole time Shirley was running for her dear life and screaming her head off, I was hot on her heels trying to catch her, screaming also out of fear. I ran track as a kid and I was the fastest kid in all of the elementary school; however, I could not catch Shirley. It took everything to catch up to her and calm her down. Thankfully the bullet had done little damage and had gone clean through her shin. Shirley and I both knew that if our dad found out, then I would be dead or wishing so. Looking back, I wonder what on earth my father was thinking allowing a loaded weapon to be in the reach of children.

After I caught up to Shirley and she stopped screaming, we had gone to our mother, who happened to come home early from work. We explained that Shirley was running around playing in the woods when Shirley fell, and a shard of glass went through her leg. My mother cleaned up the wound, and surprisingly it healed very well and very quickly. My father never found out about this. Then again, maybe he figured it out. He always seemed to be all knowing.

Although cute and funny, Shirley didn't have many friends. She wasn't allowed to go to sleepovers with the other girls or go to friends' houses to play. She had to come straight home from school and begin my father's program of doing homework, staying in the tent, and waiting for my mom to come home from work. Shirley had been allowed in the house at first, but her time outside grew more and more. Eventually, the tent in the woods became Shirley's tent. My father did not want my sister around either. Eventually he could not tolerate the stress of having her around in the house. When my mother went to work in the evening, he was in the house. I lived in the barn and Shirley lived in the tent.

Shirley didn't get a TV or radio in the tent. She spent her spare time coloring or playing with a doll in an imaginary world. I wonder if this isolation caused her to be someone who, as an adolescent and adult, begged for attention. She had to be louder than everyone else and be more dramatic. She had a very large personality and easily irritated people around her. This resonated in her behavior as she grew up.

I sustained many beatings on Shirley's behalf, but Shirley was abused also. When Shirley wet her bed, my father would hang her sheets outside her bedroom window for all to see. I am thankful we didn't live on a busy street for much of this time. Shirley suffered enough humiliation as the school bus did pass our house every morning.

Shirley never quite fit in even as an adult. She had a series of relationships, looking for love. She never had many true friends and ran amuck. She could be funny and kind, but she also had a temper and could be quarrelsome. She never raised her 2 children, and it was obvious that she had trouble bonding with them. One was adopted by my mother and stepfather and her other son was given to his father. Shirley could only care about Shirley. Her life was filled with chaos and constant moving. She left home when she was quite young, escaping a series of foster homes, only to become emancipated and move across country as a young teen of 14. She has a myriad of medical problems.

Shirley had a tumultuous relationship with my mother, and they do not speak. I think my mother loves her but doesn't particularly like her. My mother raised Shirley's son from infancy to adulthood and did so quite well. In many ways, my mother made up for the love and kindness she failed to show us. Shirley and I do not keep in touch any longer. The last time I saw her was when we settled my father's estate. I heard she is married and stable. I pray that she finds peace and happiness.

# CHAPTER 12

## *My Mother*

I love my mother, and I have always loved her. Even when she was absent, I loved her. I have very few memories of her during my childhood. It seems like she was always at work and never present. I don't know if this was physical or mental, but she was not there.

My mother was tiny in comparison to my father's six-foot frame. I had no idea at the time, but my mother had also suffered at the hands of my father. According to my mother, my father had grabbed her and pinned her in the kitchen shortly after he killed Linda. I have a faint memory of this, but children have a way of blocking out terrible things, and sometimes the memory is distorted. I was left with the impression that he was threatening her. Of course, he never showed this kind of abuse in front of Shirley or I, and so for many years I could not grasp the abuse was happening to my mother also.

I tend to question my mother's words when she tells me about the past. I never understood why my mother would not simply grab us and flee for her life after witnessing the things she did, especially after my father killed Linda. My father terrorized my mother for years and brainwashed her completely. She learned to cope by zoning out, by avoiding, and by disappearing.

My mother was married at 17 and had me when she was only eighteen years old. In retrospect, I have thought about this entire story over and over. I have come to the conclusion that my mother was just a simple naïve little girl. She got married as a means to get out of the house. It is no doubt my father saw his opportunity to control and manipulate my mother, and so he pursued her. This control also included separating my mother from her own family so he could be the monster he intended to be. None of the family knew any of this was going on. I found out later, my mother has quite the large family with multiple brothers and sisters. Knowing the things I know now, her brothers would have taken my father out to the wood-shed and given my father a beating of his own. My mother never asked for help or wanted to upset the apple cart. She was under his spell and scared to death. She may have also not wanted the big "I told you so" from her family because she married my father at age 17 and had to have her parents' legal permission to get married. When things went south, she kept it to herself and hid the problems from her family.

My childhood was so mind boggling, and I have gone over various scenarios in my head thinking about the "what if's." I do remember a time picking up my shotgun and leveling it at my father's back as he walked away. I was shaking uncontrollably and thinking to myself, "What if I miss him? I will be dead meat." I understood the power of the gun I held in my hands as I had killed my first little bird with a twenty-two. It is oddly strange how many of these incidents impacted me and my train of thought. Actually, in some odd way, it made me a better person, as I cherished life.

Now that may seem odd or funny to many, but to me a life was anything living, breathing, thinking, feeding, or simply trying to survive. Anyone can play the tough guy behind the trigger of a gun! I'm better than that and I knew it then just as I know it today.

My life was so strange back then. It seemed like no matter how wonderful something could be or no matter how much fun Shirley and I were having, something was always wrong or went wrong. Many times, I thought Shirley and I were cursed.

Once, I had shot a little bird with a twenty-two rifle. I can't remember how I got my dad's twenty-two rifle that day, but I was up behind the barn following a small flock of sparrows. The birds were sitting still when I shot one of them causing the other birds to scatter in the air. Honestly all I saw was a puff of feathers when I shot that bird, and I never actually found it. I was very saddened by and remorseful for my actions. I am not sure why I did it other than to emulate my father hunting or maybe because I was being a kid.

My mother had her own talents and love for life that she never fully got to experience until years after her divorce from my father. My memories are few and far between. Essentially all I have are snip-its of memories of her. My mother was an excellent cook. When she was home, I remember her cheerfully cooking in the kitchen. She seemed to enjoy cooking and the kitchen was her domain. She buzzed around the kitchen and did her best when she was home and had to cook, only to be shocked back into reality when my father walked in the door. She would be chopping and dicing and preparing a meal, but his mere presence stifled her immediately. She would stop dead in her tracks, and it was obvious that she could not be herself. She could not relax. She walked on eggshells just like Shirley and I did, waiting for the flip of the switch. Any evidence of even the slightest of happiness was wiped off her face.

My mother could also sew but didn't spend much time doing so. Again, I am not sure why. I don't remember any other hobbies. I honestly do not know what she did in her spare time. After leaving my father, my mother took on a new persona and showed her talents in sewing and crafting. However, back then, she was stunted. When my mother was not working, I don't remember what she was doing other than tending to my father or performing chores such as washing dishes or doing laundry. She did not have friends and had little to no contact with her family. She barely had contact with Shirley and me. What an empty, sad life.

# CHAPTER 13
## *The Final Beating*

---

This was the day that began my father's final episode that led to the end of an era of torment. My father and I got up early to go turkey hunting. I was so excited the night before that I could hardly sleep. I woke up early and was eating cereal while my father loaded the car. He had made all the preparations and got everything ready the night before.

The day started out like a normal hunting trip with excited anticipation. The day was cold, and I was prepared. We got in my father's 1965 Ford Falcon sport coupe, and I was revved up and ready to go. I loved my dad's car even though I got my little fingers locked in the car door one day, and he actually had to unlock it to get my fingers out. We went to a location he chose that wasn't far from home. I'm not sure why he picked this spot as we typically went farther into the woods to hunt. As I climbed out of the car and closed my door, I was careful not to smash my fingers again. I ran to the trunk were my dad pulled out our guns and slowly loaded them in preparation for the hunt. As he loaded my gun, he laid it back into the car trunk and pulled out his gun to load it. He returned his gun to the trunk.

What happened next caught me off guard, and I was not prepared for his outburst like I usually was. My father reached in and pulled out my gun and began beating me with it. He was shoving the butt of the gun in my face and hitting me wildly all over my body. He became so outraged so quickly and was wailing on me in a wild manner. After the first blow with the butt of the gun, I immediately hit the ground. I was in such pain and agony that I couldn't get up. He continued slamming me with the gun, and I was screaming and crying out. I was stunned and shocked as I lay on the ground doing my best to fend off the wild blows. He pounded the butt of that shotgun into my ribs, arms, back, legs, and hips.

As quickly as the beating started, it stopped. He threw the shotgun at me and hollered, "Don't you ever slam my car door like that and make so much noise while hunting with me again." He simply walked away, reached in the trunk and grabbed his gun, and ever so quietly closed the trunk of the car. He turned his back and walked away. I didn't even recall slamming the car door or making noise. I was stunned and hurt so badly. What on earth did I do? An overwhelming anger then came over me. Another awful end to a perfectly good time. Another outing ruined. In my lap lay a shotgun that could take him out. As I lay on the ground struggling to get up, I began thinking and dwelling over the possibility of shooting him. I even lifted the gun at one point and aimed it at him, thinking life would be so much better for everyone if he wasn't around. I was sad and angry at the same time. I was hurt. I knew I did not have it in me to shoot him. It would have been so easy. I look back on this today and know I did the right thing. I showed tremendous restraint, and I was the better man.

Sitting with him in the woods for the remainder of the morning was frightening, and thus I kept him in my peripheral vision. I kept quiet and at a distance so I wouldn't set him off. I remained on high alert until we left around noon. The entire morning was painful both mentally and physically. This was an absolutely miserable trip. My injuries were aching and started to swell and throb. I don't remember much after this point, as I seemed to have blacked out. I returned home only to receive another series of beatings. My father had ultimately flipped out this time, and it was bad. When we got home, he immediately started beating me. For what, I wasn't sure. I passed out.

After beating me several times, my father turned his sights on Shirley. My father beat Shirley very badly. I could not figure out what either one of us had done. He was acting very strange, unlike any other time I had ever seen. He had a wild look in his eyes. I couldn't quite put my finger on it. He had a tremendous amount of tension and anger. He was a man in a rage. He took scissors and cut Shirley's hair. He gave Shirley a bowl-shaped haircut, that was so short around the bangs and made a perfect circle around her head. The hair on her forehead wasn't even a 1/8 inch long. I honestly thought he put a bowl on her head and cut around it. He said he cut her hair because "she thought she was too cute." His hatred towards us was obvious. There was no hiding it this weekend. His strange behavior continued through Sunday, and we were terrified. I do not recall seeing my mother the entire weekend. I had mentally checked out and for all I know, she was there. I am certain I suffered a head injury. The emotional trauma was irreparable.

My father was like a rabid dog. We were doing our best to stay away. Shirley and I were severely beaten multiple times over the entire weekend. We cried and bled for hours. We could barely walk or move our limbs. His anger was insatiable. In many ways, this was his grand finale. No matter how many times he hit us or beat us, he couldn't vent his frustrations. He was sick and needed help. Shirley and I were injured and needed help.

Come Monday, my father acted like everything was normal, and we should just go on our merry way to school. On Monday morning, we could barely get up for school. We hobbled to the bus stop. I am not sure how we mustered up the strength to go to school, but we knew if we got there, then we would be safe at least for a few hours.

When we got on the bus, students immediately started picking on Shirley about her hair cut. The bus driver obviously realized something was terribly wrong. She pulled over and brought Shirley to the front of the bus and separated her from the other students. She had Shirley sit near her so she could watch her. The bus driver called ahead to the school to inform them that there was an issue with Shirley and possibly with me, because the driver saw me limping. The bus ride was a complete blur to me. I am sure I had suffered brain injuries or at minimal a concussion or two over the weekend. I sat still and motionless because every bump or turn the bus made caused me pain. I struggled to get off the bus and make my way to my home room. My entire body was beat, bruised, and battered.

I sauntered to Mrs. Compton's homeroom class for roll call. I was on autopilot at this point, just going through the motions. At some point, I heard my name over the intercom. "Would James Kramer please report to the principal's office? Thank you!" I got up like a zombie and made my way to the office. I was walking, but my mind was dwelling over the kind of problems I was going to have with my father tonight when he found out I'm in trouble at school. I could barely think straight, but I was searching my memory for anything that I possibly could be in trouble for at school.

The students in my homeroom stared at me as I got up to walk out of the classroom. All I could think was "What did I do now? What am I going to have to face when I get home?"I lowered my head in shame and made no attempt to make eye contact with anyone. I wanted to be invisible. As I walked towards the principal's office down the corridor, I walked slower and slower, pondering what was to come. When I opened the office door, the office staff stared. The silence was awkward and tense. It gave me the feeling I was a very bad, bad child.

Walking through the office door, I was directed towards the principal's office door. Upon entering, I was met by the principal and two adults in suits. I had never seen them before. The principal asked me some personal information about my home life to which I had little to no reply. I think I may have shrugged and mumbled an okay or two. I was trying to keep my life secret, particularly those events that had just taken place over the weekend.

The principal allowed me to return to class after asking me his questions. I immediately thought to myself afterward, as I walked back to class, "Wow, was that close!" When I got to my locker, I prepared myself for Mr. Reeder's English class. I could barely walk, and it was surprising that the principal even let me leave. Mr. Reeder was a very tough, firm, and stern teacher who believed in the power of education. He required that his students be attentive and alert, and also be very quiet in his class. I was extremely afraid of this man when I appeared in his class. Back then teachers had the right to physically discipline a student if they were of a nuisance in class. Mr. Reeder was known for his paddles that the woodshop students made for him, and he kept it proudly hung on the front side of his desk. I was very quiet and careful as I entered the class. After the teachers found out about the abuse Shirley and I sustained, Mr. Reeder changed toward me. I found him to be a very thoughtful, gentle, loving spirit, and he was very kind towards me.

The students knew how Mr. Reeder handled problem students, and I was no exception. He was bigger than my dad and at the time I thought just as mean. On this particular day I had trouble staying awake for most of my classes, but I was trying my best to stay alert and attentive for his class. After all I was not in the mood or physical condition for any more discipline. I was tired and hurt and really gave his class my all. By the end of his class, there was another announcement over the intercom system. "James Kramer please come to the principal's office." My heart sank. I hurried to the office this time, just wanting to get whatever it was over with. When I showed up this time, Shirley was sitting there. There were also several other people in the office including the school nurse and counselor.

This group included police officers. I also noticed State Trooper Rossetti in the crowd. I had met her before when I ran away. She was one of the troopers that spoke with my father and me. Shortly after arriving at the office, several unknown adults started looking over our exposed body parts, examining our faces, legs, and arms. They were taking notes of the bruising on our wrists and forearms. It was only obvious that something horrendous happened to us at home. I thought to myself, "Someone is not going to allow us to go back home today." This was such a humiliating experience primarily because I did not know any of these people. They inspected us as if we were merchandise and asked so many questions that they made my head spin. This was not handled in the most sensitive manner with any concern about our emotional state.

This ordeal went on for several hours. Shirley and I had no idea who these people were, and this made it quite frightening. Eventually they asked us if we would remove our clothes so they could see the other injuries. We went in the nurse's office individually where one of them took hundreds of photos. We were embarrassed, but we complied. It seemed like hundreds of photos were taken of our open cuts, bruises, and battered body parts. They also took photos of Shirley and the awful haircut. Confused and overwhelmed, Shirley and I simply could not figure out whether we should be happy, sad, or scared. What was going to happen when our father found out? His wrath will be legendary. I was silently praying we were not sent home to him. Not one of these adults did a very good job explaining the circumstances or what was happening to Shirley and I or what the plan was. We felt victimized yet again.

The only reassuring part of this ordeal was that Trooper Rossetti was one of the state troopers on the scene. She was so kind to us, and my own little boyish way I really liked her. A genuinely kind person was few and far between in my life. I felt completely safe with her close by. While all the adults were talking and taking pictures and discussing our situation among themselves, I tried to stay close to Trooper Rossetti as we shuffled from here to there.

I found out later that trooper Rossetti had attempted to keep us with her until suitable places came to light for us to stay. I also know that she was one of the officers who interrogated my father. She testified in court as to statements he had made to her about never wanting us back and never wanting kids anyway. Mrs. Hewett, Shirley's homeroom teacher intervened immediately after Shirley arrived at the school with her hair looking the way it did. Mrs. Hewett knew immediately something was grossly wrong. After all was said and done at the school, I have a block in my memory. According to the court documents, the authorities would arrest my father that day, and we went home that night. The documents said that within a week, Child Welfare had removed us and taken to the Reading Children's Home.

Honestly my memory of the things that unfolded are very blurry, and I am sure it is partly from the psychological trauma and partly from my physical injuries. My father had hit me in the head numerous times, and I had lost consciousness. I have no recollection of going to school, but according to court documents we went to school the remainder of the week. Therefore, we must have stayed with our mother. I don't remember any of this. The officers continued their investigation, and we were removed within the next few days and placed in the Reading Children's Home.

When Shirley and I had been placed in the Reading Children's Home, we were tossed in with other angry children and staff members who were not really very interested in our stories or dealing with our trauma. Within a month, Mrs. Hewett had managed to take Shirley into her care as a foster child and had Shirley stay at her house. This separated us, but I was glad for Shirley. Mrs. Hewett bought Shirley a wig to cover her haircut until her hair grew back out. She also fought to keep Shirley permanently. I missed Shirley, but I was happy for her because it seemed like she got a break. No one kept us informed as to what was happening with our parents. I had no idea what was going on with my mother. I was also worried about her because my father was a raving mad lunatic that weekend, and I didn't know if he had harmed my mother. I kept asking staff, but they did not have much information to offer.

Shirley and I did the best we could to fit in with the other kids, but always in the back of my mind I wondered about my father. Had they picked him up yet? Locked him away? What had happened to our mother? Nobody told us anything. We had no idea if any of our other family members knew about us? Did grandma know the police had taken us away? At that age I guess I could not comprehend the separation from our family, especially our mother. I'm sure there were reasons, but nothing was being provided to us. I also wondered why my grandmother or my mother's parents, or other family didn't come and help me.

In a sense, Shirley and I were imprisoned. We were tossed in an environment with troubled kids. They smoked and did drugs and we had never been exposed to this or some of their behavior. We didn't receive any counseling or care for our fragile emotional state. We had just come out of a nightmare. There was no one there to help. We only had food, shelter, and clothing. Nothing more. And, we were locked away without knowing anything about our mother or father.

Eventually, Shirley and I were told that the police arrested my father, and he was in the county jail on various charges. Surprisingly, the charges were not just those related to beating Shirley and I, but he had been charged with Linda's murder. There was a newspaper article that reported that a "Salford man was held in child's death" from seven years previous. The District Attorney intended to prosecute my father not only for our injuries but for Linda's death that occurred almost seven years earlier. At some point, I testified against him in court, pointing him out as my abuser. I don't recall any of the details or questioning related to Linda. The attorneys asked me other questions in the courtroom, especially questions about the photos that littered the prosecution's table. My mental state was simply not functioning for several months after the final beating and much of the trial has been wiped from my memory. I am often thankful for my brain's protective mechanism. I don't think I want to recall all of it. It was much too devastating.

The hundreds of photos eventually were dismissed as evidence. Other solid evidence was also dismissed. My father had a good lawyer, and he fought hard because he knew what awaited my father inside those prison walls. A man who killed a baby and then tried to beat his remaining two young children to death would not fare well. Even the correctional system has a moral code. As for me, I never wanted to see him again. I simply wanted my sister Shirley, my mother, and I to be together and to live peacefully together without him. I wanted safety and peace. I prayed to God every day.

My mother had her own issues at this point, and I hardly knew she existed. I was sad for her, and I missed her. But in retrospect, I always missed her as she was never quite in the picture. I knew she was overwhelmed with all of it. Mentally she was gone. I do not think she was capable of taking care of herself, let alone any children. For me, life simply felt like a slow-motion movie, and things were fuzzy and extremely confusing most of the time. I think my mother was probably going through the same feelings and emotional states that I was. She was lost and all alone, and no matter how much I reached out, "we" as a family would never be the same and may never exist. For the first time we could breathe and think about all the terrible things that transpired over the years. In some ways this was the path to recovery, but in other ways, it opened wounds in a deep, deep way. I wept for my mother many times. I wept for Shirley. The psychological help that was promised through the courts never came. We suffered in silence, each in our own way.

After my father's arrest, I am sure my mother played the "what if" game. She felt powerless to do anything after my father killed Linda. She was overwhelmed with sorrow, pain, shame, and humiliation. These things drove her over the edge, and in many ways, she coped by hiding or avoiding. All of our family's dirty laundry was being aired out in the open during the trial. Many fingers pointed towards my mother. People were wondering how she let this happen and questioning why she didn't get help. People wondered where she was when all the beatings took place.

I think this was my mother's breaking point, and it sent her spiraling into a mental breakdown. The questions in the courtroom lead to how Linda died, and why it took so long to get her to a hospital. She had turned a blind eye after Linda's death and turned to stone in the courtroom. They critiqued my mother and made her sound like a criminal when it was my father who was the criminal on trial. My mother was paralyzed after her daughter's death. Nothing else needs to be said.

Some of the evidence showed that if not for a neighbor talking my mother into taking Linda to the hospital, Linda would have died suffering in her crib. What would have happened then? My heart cries to this day for my mother and for Linda who suffered to her last and final breath. What a sad thing for a baby to experience before the light is taken away. What a terrible memory for my mother to have to live with all these years, before she could find the comfort of telling the story openly in court. She suffers to this day thinking about little Linda.

My father made up all kinds of stories about beating Shirley and me. He tried to explain away that it was normal discipline. He concocted a story about finding Shirley and I with a stolen bike. He felt it was his parental obligation to discipline us and teach us a lesson. However, forensic experts and physicians testified to the tremendous force of the beatings, which caused the degree of injury, particularly the ecchymosis under our skin.

My father was eventually sentenced to a measly five to fifteen years for manslaughter related to Linda's murder. He denied this too and one of the headlines in a paper quoted him as stating that "she seemed sick." He denied hitting her although the autopsy stated she died of peritonitis and the physicians stated this was caused by a blow to her abdomen. With two years of jail time served, subtracted from his sentence and running his other sentences concurrently, he would only do a minimum of 3 years. He also was convicted of several counts of battery, which held no real merit over the presiding charge of manslaughter. He was transferred to Graterford State Prison where he did his time in protective custody as a child murderer. My father was full of excuses and full of appeals. He rationalized all of his wrongdoing. My mother did stand up in court and tell the truth despite him threatening her from jail.

My mother continued to live in the old house in Salford Station as she had no other place to go. She was picking up the pieces and doing her best to get herself together. I know my father only served out another three to four years before he was released, but my mother felt some safety knowing he could not hurt her. As the end of his sentence neared, my mother sold the house and all its property. She wanted desperately to feel safe and to start a new life in Quakertown. My mother had a hard time transitioning into her new lifestyle. She was free of the terror, but she had never lived on her own. She married my father at 17 and lived in his clutches for 12 years. Now she was on her own and severely traumatized.

I'm sure my mother missed us after they took us away, at least I hope she did. Shirley and I continued in foster care because my mother thought it was the best thing at that time. She needed to reconstruct her life and make things better for herself first, with the goal of making a home for us and helping Shirley and I recover from our ordeal and the past several years of hell. My mother told us she wanted to get her life together and have us all live together again. I was counting on her.

My mother was working and reunited with family. She made a few friends and made a couple attempts at meeting other men. Her dates simply did not work out. One day, she met Leroy. Leroy was a stable, squared away, honest, hard-working, and quiet man. He was a Godsend for my mother. He helped her get back on her feet and start a new life, free of abuse. He was kind and patient. He was supportive of her, and he cared about Shirley and me.

Shirley was still with Mrs. Hewett and her family. At the time, Mrs. Hewett thought this was awesome for Shirley as it would give her a sense of normalcy and stability. My mother also thought this as well. However, Shirley thought just the opposite and that my mother simply did not care for her or want Shirley around. Shirley felt rejected and abandoned.

I was bounced around from one foster home to another as I continuously struggled to return home. My belief was that my mother missed me and wanted me home. I rejected any notion that my mother abandoned us. I missed my mother, and I wanted to be home. I wanted to be in *my* home—a place I could call my own. I wanted to be around family and people that loved me, not around people who tolerated me.

Therefore, I kept running away from the foster placements. In many ways I thought that Shirley could not grasp the gravity of the situation and how damaged my mother really was. I knew I wanted to be with my mother. I was angry and could not grasp why our mother would not bring us back home. No foster home was comfortable, so I would run away the first chance I got and attempt to return home. I was persistent. Nothing would do but being home with my mother. I could not understand and eventually began thinking she didn't want me. I grew tired of making excuses about her getting herself together.

Time passed and several years later, my mother's relationship with Leroy grew and thanks to him my mother's life stabilized. Leroy and my mother agreed that it was time for me to live with them. After she sold the house in Salford Station, I moved in. I was thankful not to return to the house where I lived in the barn like a prisoner.

After my return, I was a bit out of control and could not settle down long enough to focus. I had been bounced around so much and received no treatment. In retrospect, I was severely hurt and in dire need of therapy. I had post-traumatic stress coupled with depression. Once again, none of the adults recognized this. I was filled with anger and rage, and I was acting out. Eventually I landed myself in trouble with the law at the age of fourteen. I had been in court for running away from the foster placements and for truancy. The courts had grown tired of my ways, and so they placed me in Saint Gabriel's School for Boys in Valley Forge, Pennsylvania. Transfixed on the ability to bond with God and educate myself at the same time was a blessing. I found the Christian Brothers who ran the school to be amazing. There was discipline of course, but nothing like I had encountered. Their discipline was done with respect and kindness, not anger and rage. They taught me morals, values, and respect. I still reminisce over the days of being there. Saint Gabriel's gave me structure and provided me the solitude to think about my demons. I needed that place and felt God's hand in this.

I enjoyed the school and being around the other kids. I enjoyed the company of the brothers who maintained order and structure and lead us as excellent role models. The school often had activities throughout the day, teaching us how to get along with others and how to find worthwhile, quiet, and productive entertainment. We were able to focus on work or play. The weekend hikes were the days I enjoyed the most. The area surrounding St. Gabriel's was breathtaking, with the rolling hills of Valley Forge in the background. The summer, spring, and fall moths were the times we hiked and the times I remember best. I went back once to see its majestic halls and to be thankful for being there and to understand the Lord's path for me.

After my educational experience at St. Gabriel's Hall, I returned home thinking that I would pick up and live a somewhat normal life with my mother and Leroy. I probably should have remained at Saint Gabriel's longer or until I finished school. I'm not sure that would have been an option, but it would have been good for me. When I returned to live with my mother, I went to school and carried on as if nothing ever happened. I had no psychological counselling, and I was never evaluated medically for any sustained trauma or head injuries. I then began using alcohol and drugs. I struggled through my youth trying to ease my pain. I covered up my problems, anger, and frustrations. Many times, I struggled to remember things through the cloud and haze of chaos that took place. At times I was glad and thankful that I did not remember.

My growing desire to rebel eventually took hold, and I became less and less interested in what school had to offer and focused more on what the world could teach me. With my attitude and focus going astray, my attendance at school dwindled. First it was simply being tardy or late, and eventually I skipped school all together. I got into a destructive habit. I woke up late in the afternoon and then went to see my friends as they came home from school. Locking myself in my bedroom, I slowly isolated myself from my mother and Leroy. As much sleep as I was getting and with loss of interest in the things, I enjoyed the most. I stopped taking hikes and spending time outdoors, I grew more and more depressed. The therapy never occurred. No one ever asked me what was wrong. The mental recovery and psychological work I needed to recover never took place. I coped with my PTSD by first being depressed, then by becoming rebellious.

I had years of pent up anger. My mother was around but did not talk much about my issues. Anything I did wrong, she responded by either ignoring me or telling me she was going to kick me out. She never talked about anything related to my angst or troubles. I think she was still in denial or using her usual ways of avoiding problems all together. After numerous absences from high school, I was expelled. I was so terribly bored and frustrated. No one ever asked me what was going on. I hated life. I was still angry about what my father had put us through. At 15, I was old enough to see the potentially good life we could have had as a family, and the severe destruction my father caused, and I was mad.

Instead of dealing with the real problems, I transferred to another school. Shortly after, I quit because I thought I would be able to go to work. I thought having a job would lead to my freedom, and I wanted my own money. I wish someone would have intervened. At the age of 15, I did not know that viable employment was not an option, and my plans were not realistic. I became a handful with a rebellious nature. I stayed out late, partying with friends, and I simply did not care much about anything. I was living moment to moment. My mother reached a point in which she could not handle the situation. She threw me out of the house just before my sixteenth birthday. For the first time ever, I found myself alone, hungry, and of course without money to support myself. I had no shelter and thus I took up sleeping in my car for the first few weeks or so.

Leroy was kind and thoughtful and previously purchased a 1971 Chevy Nova for me in preparation of getting a driver's license. Even though I didn't have a license, Leroy thought it would cheer me up and get me back and forth to a decent job. Thankfully, the Nova gave me a roof over my head. Living in the car was tough with my personal belongings crammed in such a small place, but I made it work. The Nova was certainly compact, but they were cheap on gas and offered me a place of shelter.

After being kicked out at 15, I did not have many options. This is where life took another downward turn. I am not proud of some of the things I did, but I was in survival mode. I did what I had to do to live. I couldn't find a job at 15 with no experience and no education. I stole food to live. I typically took food from businesses. I also stole money if the opportunity presented itself. I never used force, and I only took things I truly needed to live. I never took anything of value as I had no need for it. My acts were purely based on survival. For the next year, I did things that I had no idea would catch up to me nearly six years later, when I turned twenty-one. In the meantime, I continued to try to live. I abandoned my car and went on the road headed west. This was the upside to being thrown out. I was on my own. I got what I wanted. I had freedom. This time, I was no longer confined or trapped. In some ways, I believe I was trying to undo the years I spent locked under the control of my father, living in a barn in which every move, every breath, and every action was closely scrutinized and controlled. The years I spent unloved, trapped in a barn.

Most of my life experience, I gained by traveling back and forth from Santa Barbara, California to Quakertown, Pennsylvania. I also traveled as far south as I could going into Florida and Texas. I didn't spend much time in the South as a teenager. I preferred California as I found many people just like me. I stayed to myself most of the time. I found that it was fun to travel the road. I put together my pack. After a while I had a back-pack, bedroll, canned goods, and the utensils I needed to eat or cook. I was independent and living free. I enjoyed being on the open road—no hurries, no place to be, no place to go. I was in control of my destiny and had no one ready to beat me or monitor my every move. Although there were inherent dangers to being on the road, I learned to be street smart. I wasn't scared of the night or being alone. This was a reprieve from the nights living under my father's control. I now had peace in an odd way. I also believe that God watched out for me and protected me.

I travelled to several cities and enjoyed this beautiful country. I learned how to live minimally and be thankful for even the smallest of things. At some point, the only problem was I was still truly alone. The loneliness only bothered me on occasion. At one point I even lived in a multimillion-dollar home in Santa Barbara with a teenage friend I had met. His mother allowed me to stay as long as I acted as a caretaker for the property. The house was like nothing I had ever seen with over 5,000 square feet and high cathedral ceilings and expansive windows. It was only a block from the beach, where we could go and hang out every day. Eventually that fell through when his mother's property was foreclosed on, but it was wonderful while it lasted. After traveling for the next couple of years, I had grown weary. In many ways, living on the road can be a hard life. I had to worry meal to meal and watch the changing weather to protect myself from the elements. For example, I could not be travelling through Montana in fall in case of a snow storm and had to stick to certain areas during particular seasons. I had to worry about strangers. I was cautious around older people and stayed away from homeless camps or people drinking and doing drugs. I stayed clear of law enforcement or anyone that could cause me trouble.

One day, I had enough. I called Leroy and asked him if I could come home. I was seventeen and believed I could get a job, do my best to get myself together, and move on. Leroy welcomed me back. When I got home, I took a job working for Spinlon Industries on Fifth Street in Quakertown. This was an entry-level position but gave me money and self-esteem.

As I turned eighteen, I wanted more for myself. I was a hard worker and had a strong work ethic. After I proved myself to Leroy, he helped me get a job at the steel plant where he worked. He had been a loyal and dedicated employee at the plant for many years and had an outstanding reputation. I wanted to make him proud of me. I was so excited at the thought of working there. I was ecstatic at the thought of working with Leroy.

The Arco Steel Plant was just outside of Souderton, Pennsylvania and close to where we lived. When I got the job, I was thrilled. This was a boost to my ego, and I really needed this. I enjoyed working in the plant, and it was a pleasure to work with Leroy, whom I became closer to as the months rolled past. I thought that working at the plant was actually fun and the hours, benefits, and pay where fantastic, particularly at my age. When I described the work as "fun," people stared at me. I enjoyed working with my hands in a physical job. This was a very demanding job, and I soon found myself growing in physical size. My muscle mass was growing. I felt more confident. I found a sense of gratitude. I was also appreciated for a job well done which in turn gave me more confidence. I enjoyed being around adults and being treated like an adult. I learned a lot about being responsible and being a team member. Soon I was cashing my check and saving money. I started taking hundred-dollar bills and putting them into my own personal record collection and savings. I would give my mother money, and then I would purchase two special record albums including many "live" versions with two to four sleeves. These were the more expensive and collectible versions. I had a nice stereo and enjoyed listening to my very special music collection. I found that I did not like banks. Therefore, I created my own savings account. I would place a hundred-dollar bill in each album. This not only became a very special music collection with rare and valuable records, but also my banking system.

Before I left on the road at age 15 and was still in high school, I had met two very good friends. These friendships would be lifelong. I met Duane in the auto shop. We hit it off immediately and just seemed to be like brothers. Duane was big and bear-like but had the funniest sense of humor. He would do outrageous things to make people laugh and be the life of the party. We understood one another, enjoyed the same things in life, and generally got along. Glenn was another very good friend whom I met over the years by just hanging out. Together, we also formed a lasting bond of brotherhood. Glenn was a solid guy with good looks and charm.

He was bright, sensible, and stable. The girls loved him. Back in these days, we were all about fun.

When I returned to Quakertown, we would get together. So, when I came back and started work at the plant, we all reunited. The fun times began again. We loved to hang out and find adventures. We also got together to party. The drinking age was twenty-one in Pennsylvania and eighteen in many of the eastern states closest to us. Therefore, we would travel to New Jersey to get beer for our weekend festivities. The three of us stuck together over the years, and of course made many friends along the way. When I was on the road, I missed them. When I returned to live with my mom and Leroy and go to work at the steel plant, I was more than happy to reconnect. I fell into a routine of going to work at the plant and meeting up with them or my girlfriend to party or have excursions.

Our parents knew one another, so there was never a problem with hanging out with each other. After I started working at the steel plant, I seemed to have everything, and life was peachy for once. I had wonderful friends, an awesome car, a savings, and a terrific girlfriend. Unfortunately, drinking led to indulging or dabbling in drugs, which can lead one down a terrible path. Of course, I landed myself in trouble with the law. I had never been treated for all of the trauma I experienced and despite everything looking normal on the outside, it wasn't on the inside. I felt guilty about my past and stealing from others when I was on the road as a teen. At one point, I was confronted by the police for drugs and I spilled the beans on myself. For some strange reason, I told the police about stealing when I was 15 and living on the streets. I had some strange, child-minded belief that the criminal justice system would be lenient on me for being honest. I thought getting this off my chest would be freeing. I found myself purging, like a confessional. What I needed was a lawyer. Telling everything to the police like I was in confession was definitely not how the system worked. In this regard, I was naïve. I thought they would understand that I was trying to survive at the age of fifteen and needed to get that off my chest. They somehow took this information and pinned several burglaries on me that I honestly did not do. The statute of limitations was up for the thefts I committed when I was 15, but somehow that was not applied to me. I was wrongfully charged as an adult at age 21 of things I had done as an early teen.

At age 21, depression set in very quickly as I watched everything I had in my life dwindle away. I lost everything. I'd lost touch with my friends and my girlfriend. I lost my mother and Leroy. I could not wrap my brain around what had occurred, and my attorney was no help whatsoever. I did not understand how this could happen. I didn't understand how my trouble was over food and necessities I had taken when I was so very young and dumb as part of my survival. This was impossible. How could I be so naïve? I often wonder if I didn't subconsciously sabotage my life. I put myself back in that barn, although now instead of a barn it was a cell. Instead of my father towering over me waiting to pounce, it was a guard.

My mother said good riddance. She thought nothing of losing me. She thought nothing of my belongings and simply gave everything away. Not knowing my savings was tucked away in those albums, she gave away all my records. In those records, was thousands and thousands of dollars. She sold my beautiful 1970 ½ Camaro. Not only did I lose everything I loved and enjoyed, I was propelled into a downward spiral. I know these were only material things, and as I would grow older, I would learn that objects come and go. But these were possessions I had worked hard for that symbolized that I was making something of myself. I was proving my father wrong. He had told me so many times that I would never amount to anything, would never have anything, and would be worthless. I had pulled myself out of the pit of hell after the horrible life with my father and being bounced from foster care to foster care, to another pit of hell. How was I going to mentally survive being locked up?

Well, I survived. I have a certain amount of PTSD related to this, but it is all one intertwined mess. If I survived my father, I realized I could survive anything. I prayed to God and I used my time wisely. I used every opportunity to improve myself. I worked out. I did art work. I read. I prayed. I pulled every bit of inner strength I had left to survive.

After a couple years, I was free. I changed and matured. I found that not many people could understand the things I had been through or why I did the things I did. I could not return to my home town. I was at a crossroads. How could I walk proudly with the thought of shame? Once again, I was a reject of sorts, all alone and deeply depressed. Trying my best to mend my life after this mess, I moved to Lompoc, California for a change of scenery and a fresh start. Jobs of course seemed hard to find and keep, and my attitude did not help. I still had not received any treatment. My PTSD was running amuck. I used alcohol to forget. I would often drink to point of no return. I found myself at that very dark place God does not wish us to go. I hated my life, I hated myself, and I felt betrayed by the system. Hey, where was that therapy? There was no recovery.

My father's words continued to repeat in my head and cut through me like a sharp utility knife. I felt like this was a self-fulfilled prophecy. Time and time again my life just never seemed to regain momentum. "You'll never be anything, and you're so ugly nobody will ever care about you or want you." I found myself drinking to drown out those words. Nothing has ever subdued this ugliness that he programmed into my head. His words still continue to trouble me to this very day. Because of God and my relationship with Him, I have never given up faith or hope and just kept trying.

I found that as an adult, I tend to want to control situations. I have a need to supervise everything, all day long, every day. This is the result of my father's programming. He would supervise me all the time, minute by minute, day after day. Never was there a break in his hovering over me. His programming is something I can't seem to shake or break, no matter what I try to do. I'm compelled to watch over my family and supervise them, continuously commenting on their actions or moves. I have contained myself and have connected that behavior to hurting them. After all these years, I continue to do my very best to stop this behavior, understand it, think about it, process it, and end it. I hate that I have many of the same behaviors as my father.

Struggling over my issues each and every day has become a haunting life experience. Each day I fight to rid this man's mental programming from my life or to erase the messages he formed in my mind. In all the years I have travelled extensively throughout the United States, on foot, by car, and by flight. Never had I found a place I could call home. Never was I comfortable in life, always shuffling from one place to another. Never keeping a job very long because of the alcohol abuse. Unable to keep friends or employment because of low frustration tolerance.

Over the years from the very start, I felt scared and alone. I never wanted to admit it. I was scared in the barn in the care of my parents. I was scared in the foster homes in the care of God knows who. One of my healthier outlets was exercise and weight lifting. I found these helped me vent frustrations. I was very athletic and well built. Some people told me I should become a professional weight lifter and go to competition. When I was in school, I excelled in track and gymnastics. I won medals and broke records. Why didn't I take this seriously and pursue this talent? My artwork also allowed me to express myself and to vent frustration. I excelled at both. As a teenager I learned I could draw and that I was especially talented. I often used this to cope. I had built a portfolio ranging from large professional drawings to doodling. I had art teachers take my work into their classes and use them to teach. They encouraged me to seek this out as a profession. I took none of this to heart. I let these escape me. In my mind, my thoughts somehow went back to my father telling me how good he was at everything, and how bad I was and how nothing I did was right. I could hear him saying that I would never amount to anything. Then at some point, whatever progress or success I was achieving, I would simply give up. I still don't quite understand why, other than that I was programmed to give up.

I've been brief about my story after my age of twenty-one, mostly because of the shame I carry with me. There was a time in my life that I did not respect or treat people fairly or righteously. This, of course, is not the person I am today and when I look back or think about the past, I have great shame. I've asked God to help transform me and to forgive me. I believe He has. I know we are all sinners, and I know my actions were wrong. I was a child and not a man. I was developmentally stunted in some strange way until I was 40. So young, so twisted, for so many years. How is this all possible? Only with the grace of God.

At the age of around thirty-two, I become involved with a woman who I thought loved me. I loved her and as rocky as our relationship started, we had two children. My daughters were the apples of my eye. I understood I had an obligation to love, respect, and care for our little girls and their mother. Things had not worked out quite as expected. I was a stay home dad for a while. I had some excellent jobs and contributed to the household. Many were seasonal, and I worked off and on, but had tried to get on disability because I found that I was experiencing difficulty working 40+ hours per week. I had physical ailments that I wouldn't learn until many years later were progressive and debilitating. I also had severe PTSD; I had difficulty interacting and communicating with others and handling large crowds.

Throughout the years, I noticed that women who are victims of child abuse are more prone to obtain assistance. Men don't complain and resources for male survivors are far more limited. I was fortunate to find a psychologist that took an interest in me and wanted to help me. He said he saw that I really needed help. My psychologist, Joel, helped me recover. I started to actually get the therapy I needed. He also helped me obtain paperwork, so I could obtain treatment and SSI. With Joel's help I was now making some headway, and he not only became my therapist but my friend. He was shocked that I had struggled so long without treatment. He knew I was a survivor and had done my best, but the road ahead was still long.

Treatment did not last. One sad day, Joel went up to "the pass" off Hwy 154 outside Santa Barbara, climbed onto the high bridge, standing backwards, he fell to his death. His suicide was mind boggling. I am at a loss for words, I lost a very good friend that day. I don't know why he committed suicide. I can only speculate. The only therapist that truly helped me was dead. He did the very thing that he encouraged me not to do. This was a great setback. I thought long and hard that there may be no hope for me and any real chance at success was doomed or jinxed. Maybe my father was right?

Honestly, I can't say I have not been close to this demise myself as the burden can be extremely heavy at times. I have always felt that suicide is the wrong way out, the coward's way. God frowns on this type of action and thus this is what has kept me going all these years. When I look back, I can see that God has always been there for me. Life is short enough already, so whatever your burden, I learned to turn to God for help.

With just under two years of therapy with Joel, and shortly after his death, my relationship with my girlfriend also dwindled. Instead of dragging out the drama in court, I opted to simply walk away. My girlfriend and I fought more and more as the relationship wore on. In many ways, I see now that I know more about abuse, that she was mentally abusive towards me. Granted, I was not always kind with my words, but I was trapped into a relationship where she controlled me and used guilt about the children to render me helpless. She knew I loved them more than anything. She used what she knew about my history and upbringing against me as a weapon. She would get angry and hit me on a couple of occasions during a bout of yelling and screaming. Many times, I did nothing. I never hit back. The storminess of this relationship peaked, and I eventually left. Her calculating nature and how she had treated men in prior relationships led me to believe that I was or would be her next victim and would wind up arrested on contrived charges if I did not leave. I also found out she was cheating. At a minimum, she was positioning herself for the next man in her life. I thought long and hard and came to the conclusion that sometimes people are just not meant to be together. Nothing could ever prepare me for the crushing blow to my heart when it came to the loss of both my daughters. She completely took them from me and would not let me see them. I spent almost every waking hour with them for six years—caring for them, loving them, and sharing life with them. I enjoyed every moment with them. The first Christmas apart, she would not even accept the children's Christmas presents. She had destroyed what little I had left.

The separation from them instantaneously threw me into a deep depression. There is no way to describe the loss of children due to someone else's selfishness or inconsideration. With my heart crushed to pieces, I started drinking heavily. I began consuming a fifth of whiskey or more a day. Beer was simply not enough to cover the pain. The term "drowning your sorrows" was most appropriate here. Needless to say, I'd usually pass out, wake up, never remembering a thing and starting the process all over again. I never indulged in alcohol to hurt others. It was a dulling agent. Something that helped me forget. Somehow throughout my life, I believed that God was watching over me, keeping me from harm. I thank God who was always and continuously in thought and prayer, even during my lowest points.

I dwelled over some of my past relationships. I can't imagine how anyone could live with me as I have mood swings and get easily frustrated, in a very similar way as my father. However, I have been stronger in containing myself from lashing out. With the grace of God, once again I pulled myself together.

I made several attempts to see the girls and or bring them gifts. Frustrated over being denied seeing them, I simply gave up and walked away. I closed that door as if it was another chapter in my life and I need not deal with it again. Sometimes I worry I am pretty heartless when I think it over. The more I dwell on something, the heavier it is on my heart, my thoughts, and my health. I learned the ability to shut off those feelings years ago during the beatings, the burning of toys, the lack of hope,

the ruin of dreams and fun times, and Linda's death. I am able to discon-
nect, and this is exactly what I did. I moved on. Attempts to reconnect
with them years later were filled with pain and angst, mostly contrived by
their mother.

After living on my own for about two years, I came out of my troubled state. My drinking was less and less. I worked in construction and
remained in the Lompoc area. I eventually met a woman whose company
I enjoyed. We both had a way of speaking to one another, exchanging
smart comments. We had fun. Our exchanges were kind of cute at first,
and of course we took a shine to one another. We spent the next few years
together, and after a couple years, we had a baby. My girlfriend was not in
great health and had a chronic debilitating disease. She was also a heavy
smoker. Our baby girl was born prematurely at about 3 pounds.

I was excited to have another opportunity at fatherhood. From the
first time I set eyes on my baby girl, I loved her with all my heart. She was
so tiny in my great big hands, and I was so scared to touch her or hold her
at first for fear I'd hurt her.

After her birth, my girlfriend and I began arguing. We clashed continuously. The relationship deteriorated rapidly over a number of reasons,
some which had to do with her son from a previous relationship. She had
never officially been divorced from her husband but had full custody of
her son. He was nine and tried desperately to make me his father. I tried to
hang in there and make it work. He had behavior problems, which made
life difficult. I was miserable, unhappy, and fairly close to death's door. I
felt as though I was dying inside. I honestly felt like my spirit's light was
going out. I was not really living, but simply going through the motions.
For the first time in my life, I honestly thought I was not going to make it.
My physical health was deteriorating. I was not eating healthy. No matter
what I did, I couldn't make life better. I wanted to be dead. I did my best
to go fishing and go for hikes and have some mental reprieve, but nothing
worked. I begged God to lead my way.

My girlfriend and I fought continuously in front of the kids, and after a while, I did my best to stay clear of her. I already knew that this is not the kind of environment a child should have to cope with, so once again I simply got up and walked away. This was not easy because I loved and adored my daughter. She was around 2 years old and as cute as can be. I always made sure she had food and clean diapers. I cleaned the house and kept things in order. My girlfriend had serious issues of her own, but I could not be around her any longer.

The fondest of all my memories with my little girls was when they hugged me. Nothing in the world can express the momentary feeling in that embrace of true love. It is genuine and honest. It moved my heart and took my breath away. To me, my children had a healing power for me, and I'd grab them and squeeze them every chance I got. I enjoyed watching them explore and found their curiosity amazing. This brought me joy. I also had patience with them because I would not repeat the cycle. I prayed each day that they would grow up and have a wonderful life, the life that I did not have.

I decided that the only way I could survive was to leave this situation. Living the way I was living was going to kill me. As a result, I decided to break off the relationship and move. The fighting was at a feverish pitch. After I left, I tried hard to keep in touch, sending gifts and letters. The contact was not reciprocated. After a series of moves, I lost touch and gave up trying. I thought every day about my baby girl. Due to the dysfunction, there was no way to balance a continued relationship. The memory of running back and forth in the hospital from my girlfriend's bedside to the baby's nursery to see my tiny sweet little baby, cuddle her so closely, feed her when she needed it, will forever be with me. Without details of the dysfunctional relationship with her mom, I will just say that when my baby girl turned two, I had enough and left.

I am sorry that I could not be there as part of raising them, but I felt it best for all involved. After repeated attempts to rekindle relationships, I can say I have made a decision to cut ties. I still love my daughters, but we will not have a relationship. They have been brainwashed to believe what they believe and despite numerous attempts to reconnect, it has not worked. Their mothers weaponized this love. I cannot be repeatedly victimized again and again. There is some strange dynamic in which my daughters manipulate and lie to me and want to use me, not love me. When I've met them, they instantly start asking for things or play out some drama. They don't understand where I've been nor do they care. They have been told untruths about my past and that I was a bad person, not a good person who has had bad things happen to him. I've learned truth in the saying, "Love makes time pass, just as time makes love pass." Sad, painful, and crushing, but the truth.

I do believe my children were cheated out of knowing their father, much as I was cheated out of knowing them. I may have made poor choices in my life, but those can't be changed. There is nobody to blame as it takes two to complete a relationship. I focus on the outcome, the beauty of it all, my three girls. I can only wish them well, pray they are always happy, and ask God to bless them.

I was slow in maturing over the years, being wild, reckless, uncaring in my ways. My education did not only come from books but real-life events. Traveling all over the United States, meeting diverse people, and going through all the relationship challenges has taught me that material things are not important. Over the years I watch the news, hear it on TV or the radio about some heinous crime committed by some animal, only to lean back on the psychological excuse of bad childhood upbringing. This infuriates me. Abuse is not a reason or an excuse.

After my own upbringing I find no excuse for anyone to act out as they do and blame it on their childhood upbringing. We learn right from wrong, but some people have a flaw and have no conscience. Thankfully, I wasn't one of them. Because of my experience with pain, suffering, and mental and physical torture, I do not wish this on anyone else.

After leaving this irreconcilable situation, I met a wonderful woman. We met in California, but ironically are both from Pennsylvania. We had a great deal in common and liked many of the same things. She told me that my Pennsylvania accent was somehow calming to her and reminded her of back home. She had moved from Pennsylvania when she was 21 but has wonderful memories of growing up there. We traveled back there together and had a 3-week road trip that was unbelievably fun and in many ways an attempt at healing. We visited the house in Salford Station. We went to the barn, although I did not go in, I stood outside of it for a picture. We stayed with my mother for part of the trip. My mother went with us to Salford Station and she was very upset on the property. She said the place gave her the creeps, and we could see she was visibly shaken by being there.

My wife and I were together nine years before we were married. She is the first person I ever wanted to marry because she is one of the most incredible people I have ever met. She is spiritually uplifting. With her I found kindness, stability, and a place I could call home. We are best friends, and I am so grateful to God for sending me an angel. My time with her is an honor, and I am happily humbled in her presence. She is my gift from God, and she is there when I was at my weakest moments. Treasured forever I love her so very dearly.

She has never used my history to hurt me, only to help me. Today I live with certain medical conditions that have slowly taken away my ability to enjoy life to its fullest. My wife strongly encouraged me to seek medical care, which I have only received sporadically throughout my adult life. After finally seeing the proper specialists, I found that I have chronic pain and issues with my joints, hip, and back related to chronic debilitating illnesses. Some of this may be related to prior trauma. I had a stroke a couple years ago. I have deformities in the arches of my feet. Since I've obtained medical coverage in the past couple years, I've made some progress. And I am thankful. However, I wonder if some of this isn't related to the beatings. I am stubborn and have a hard time heeding to my doctor's requests. I am supposed to take it easy on my body parts, with no bending, lifting, heavy exercise or stress on my joints. Through all this, I had pursued my martial arts and am close to a 3rd degree Black Belt.

For the last 16 years or more, I've been studying mixed martial arts. I have always lifted weights. I also did quite a bit of hiking. The outdoors has always been a comfort and a blessing. Being with my wife fishing, walking on the beach, or running my dogs are most relaxing. I find it hard to just lay down and quit despite some of the physicians telling me to stop. So, I keep going. My wife and I spend a lot of time enjoying the forest, beaches, rivers, and anywhere we can find peace or the road takes us.

My father passed away a couple years ago. Before he died, I had the opportunity to communicate with him through the mail. Over the past years, since he was first incarcerated, my mother, sister, and I were told he was looking for us. This would cause immediate fear in all of us. At one point, he found Shirley and tried to coerce Shirley into giving up our mother's address for money. This was all before the internet, when it was more difficult to track people down. All three of us would occasionally receive odd hang-up calls.We often speculated it was him. At times, we would hear a rumor that he had remarried or had children and was doing what he did to us all over again. These notions all proved to be false. In the end, he was a lonely, solitary man, living a hermit's life.

I don't remember who made first contact, but I had a PO Box because I still did not want my father to know where I lived. He had made statements long ago that he wanted us dead. I didn't really believe that after all these years. My father's first letter to me was that of kindness, asking forgiveness but seeking information about my sister and my mother's whereabouts. I honestly think he wanted to apologize, but I couldn't be sure. I never told him anything or trusted him. Even though he was now in his 70s, I knew of his history and his mental issues. He tried to intimidate me in his letters, but it did not have any impact on me this many years later. I am not that little boy in the barn. I was an adult, and thus I told him how things really are and would be. I explained he could not hurt me anymore.

I told him I would love to try to understand him and possibly get to know him. I wanted him to know that in my heart I had forgiven him. Through my relationship with God, my anger towards him had dissipated and that I found I would never get anywhere without letting it go. I found freedom in forgiveness.

I advised my father that he must come clean with God, admit his sins and ask for forgiveness in order for me to see him again in heaven. My father said he had and sent me materials from Billy Graham ministries. My father wanted me to know that he was saved. In his own way, my father tried to show me he was making attempts to give back by donating money and giving blood and doing what he could as a man in his 70s. Only God, however, knows what is in someone's heart. It is not for me to judge or determine whether he was saved.

For some reason, I wanted to talk to my father. I wanted to stay in touch with him and keep our conversations positive. I think I was trying to figure him out. I wanted to know what he was about. I wanted to try to figure out why he did what he did, but even more so, how far he really came. Even after all these years, we both had many of the same interests and hobbies. He was truly intelligent and quite an interesting person. I knew that we may have things in common, but I would not have ever allowed him to be around children. Before he died, he sent me a couple coins from his collection and an article about his father. He was proud of his veteran father, who spent his entire life in the military. My father held this service to our country in high regard. After all these years, it was apparent my father still looked up to his dad. This actually made me a little sad, as I still wondered what the truth was about their relationship.

I could tell my father was getting old, and I even questioned his physical health. His handwriting was that of an old person's. His cursive was squiggly and shaky. He no longer had the steady artist's hand he once had, painting those tiny pictures and tying flies. Occasionally I would receive a card from him, or he would put a $20 bill in a letter. Then one day, out of nowhere, he said he would prefer to communicate once a year because it wasn't so hard on him. I found that very odd. As soon as we developed a relationship, it ended. He passed away shortly after. I don't know what was wrong with my father, but I'm sure he had some type of mental illness. He couldn't stand closeness, giving love or being loved. He had a very limited tolerance.

My father died of end stage renal disease. He was found on the floor, frozen in place. It was winter in Pennsylvania, and the pipes of his home had burst and frozen. He died cold and alone on the floor of his house. I cry every time I think of this. This is not a memory I want to hold onto or want seared in my mind. The manner of his death was so tragic. Shortly after his death, I went back to Philadelphia to deal with his estate. This was very painful, and I had to interact with Shirley. The entire handling of the estate was a struggle. If it weren't for my mother, I wouldn't have even found out he passed away. Shirley had been contacted by police but never contacted me. She hired a lawyer and tried to start the probate process without including me. This is where we parted ways. She was interested in my father's monetary value. I was not. I hired an attorney back in Pennsylvania to act on my behalf as co-executor.

When he passed away, my wife suggested planting a tree in his memory since there would be no funeral. We both agreed that that was something positive. While I was digging in the yard, I experienced the strangest occurrence. I found a flat river rock, approximately 8 inches wide with a white painted dove of peace. I took it in the house, and we were both astonished. How on earth this would appear in our backyard where there were no rocks. We had lived there 10 years and never saw this before. We had done landscaping and never dug this up. I took the rock and repainted the dove and put my father's name on the rock. I keep it with the palm tree I planted for him. One of God's mysteries, I guess. My wife tells me she feels my father is watching down from heaven and has a strange sense he is there. She calls him by his middle name "Delmar," which I find endearing. It makes me laugh when we travel, and she sees that name on street signs and various other places because it is such an unusual name. She points them out to me and says, "Look, there's Delmar." My wife says she would have loved to meet him to figure out how his mind worked. After all, my wife worked as a psychiatric nurse for part of her career.

My relationship with my mother is very hit or miss. I have tried over and over to establish communication with her. She seems mostly to tolerate me rather than love me. Although she says she loves me, she is not good at showing it. I have also tried very hard to figure her out. She did a wonderful thing by adopting and raising my sister's son. My sister was not capable of taking care of herself at the time, let alone raising a child. My mother and Leroy were wonderful parents to my nephew.

Over the past few years, my mother won't call me. I always have to call her. It is hurtful, and I've talked to her about this. It feels like I am always chasing her. Many years ago, she told me I looked like my father and it bothered her. I think this is why she avoids me. Then again, maybe not. It might just be me trying to find a tangible reason for her behavior. Her history of avoidance is proven. This is how she copes. I love my mother, and I wish things were different. Our trip to visit her was very enjoyable. She made my wife and I a beautiful handcrafted wedding gift. She seems to find enjoyment doing crafts.

During our visit, we spent many hours staying up late and talking. However, my mother still holds so much anger towards my father, even after his death. I have tried to support her and offer that letting go of the anger is the only means to move on. She cannot do this, but I continue to pray. I know how much pain she suffered and that losing a child is something that one will never truly recover. However, forgiveness is the way to freedom.

# EPILOGUE

When I wrote this book, I wanted to accomplish a few main objectives. I wanted to purge the past and continue to move forward. I also wanted to send a message to others about prevention and how to be alert for signs of an abuser. I wanted to give advice on how to help those who were or knew someone in an abusive situation. I also wanted to help people who suffered from toxic childhood stress as adult survivors of abuse. The mental and physical effects are devastating and progressive. I also wanted to find help for myself to finish the healing process and de-program my mind. I hope and pray to continue my personal healing and possibly find a therapist that can help de-program me. This has been a life-long mission, and I will not give up.

It was important for me to wait before opening up this story to the public's eyes. I did not want my words to harm my father while he lived out his final days. As I neared the end of my writing, my father passed away. Strange as it may be, I miss him and wish we had had more time together as adults to get to know one another. Maybe part of it isn't that I miss him so much as I yearn for having a father or I miss the good times we had. I find comfort knowing that my true father is the Lord God.

I hope my father understood and knew in his heart when he died that I loved him, felt sad for him, and hurt by him all at the same time. I felt sad that he ruined his life. He could have had it all. Seeing old pictures, I often study his face and wonder if he knew he had a mental illness and had any true remorse for his actions. I often wonder if he had any self-control at all. He had so much potential for happiness with a sweet wife who would have done anything for him, three lovely children, wonderful career potential, a loving mother, and a home. All my anger, frustration, and hatred for him vanished when I forgave him. It was a burden that long needed lifting. His grave marker is a stone with a dove flying off into the clouds painted on it perched under a newly planted palm tree. In many ways this is symbolic. He suffered an extremely painful death, some might say it was karma. He suffered for hours if not days on the hallway floor, alone! I wept for him then and still do now when I think of him.

Since sharing my life with my wife Judy there has come a peace within me. I still need therapy, and what I refer to as "de-programming." I feel like there is something wrong with me that I cannot fix. I have had the pleasure of a sense of calm in my heart and a general peace and solitude. My issues related to years of PTSD occur occasionally. I know that there are long term, serious effects from toxic childhood stress. More are being discovered about effects on heart disease, depression, incarceration, stroke, and suicide to name a few.

When I have an episode or flashback, I am either withdrawn and depressed or very irritable. I get moody like my father, but I have learned to handle these episodes in my own way. I also find myself being critical and a perfectionist with some difficulty handling frustration. I hate these traits in me. They are similar to my father, and I wish I could rid myself of them. I have gotten control of these most times through prayer, my martial arts, spending time outdoors, and staying physically active and busy. I do my best to identify triggers such as noise or multiple stressors occurring concurrently.

Writing this book was very hard on me, but it was therapeutic. I had frequent episodes and terrible flashbacks, and I was often very moody. I cried and was angry. I relived many of the events. I cannot even read certain parts of this book, particularly about my sister Linda and her death. I relate the writing of this book to sucking venom and sting out of a tragedy. The pain and hurt will always be in my thoughts and part of my emotional makeup. I don't think I will every completely shake it. Sometimes I experience these episodes in waves. But then there are days it just downpours on me. The programming remains. My thoughts come flooding back, and I think I am not allowed to have joy or have compliments or gifts because I am that little boy in the barn who doesn't deserve anything good.

I avoided writing this book because I knew what this would dredge up. I have avoided seeking out a therapist in the last few years because I must have the right person. I am leery about rehashing all of these painful events. It comes down to trust. After having a good relationship with Joel and feeling like I was making some progress, he killed himself. This was not good for someone like me who has serious and ingrained trust issues.

After almost forty years, I made a choice to sit and write. If not for the book to be published, for my own sanity and healing. The better part of my youth was destroyed, with no opportunity to reclaim the things I so much wanted to do in life. I feel I have never received justice. I believe the authorities, or the adults involved with my family such as Child Welfare and even family members simply ignored the situation or shuffled me around, never supplying me with real support or psychological help of any kind. Even though the court had ordered psychological help, my mother didn't pursue it for us. None of the foster homes or schools obtained this for me. The Brothers at Saint Gabriel's tried, but their job was not psychotherapy. Their job was to get me in line and back on track.

I want to leave this book with the advice that if anyone is ever in a situation like mine, please run, scream, and get help. There are many more resources today than back then. For parents that are trapped in abusive relationships, do the same. Stand up for your children. There are many more opportunities today to get help. People should be not trapped in a world controlled by another person, particularly an abuser. Today as opposed to the 1960s, much more attention has been placed on abuse. Teachers, health care providers, and first responders have been educated on signs and symptoms, and they been made mandatory reporters in most states. If all else fails, go to a Fire Station or emergency room. Call 911. Tell a teacher, a nurse, or a doctor.

For those adults who continue to suffer from past childhood toxic stress and abuse, reach out. Get counseling. I hope you eventually find peace through forgiveness. Letting go is the only path to moving on. Remember it is a long, arduous process. Be mindful and work on personal insight so you do not repeat the cycle. Do not avoid your childhood but confront it. Dig deep and find kindness and love. Never give up. Remember that you did not cause your childhood abuse. You can control your destiny. Find your triggers and ways to cope. Build a solid support system and surround yourself with positive people who do not use your past as a weapon. I know I am a survivor. My faith in God has sustained me.

I cannot conclude this book without huge thanks to my wife, who inspired me to write this story, helped me to stand firm in doing so, and stood beside me when I could not handle the pain. My wife has helped change my way of thinking and living. Without her kindred spirit, my spirit would still be lost. Thank you, my angel, for opening my eyes and helping me see things that I was blind to for so many years. I will always love you. I even struggle with our love because I feel I don't deserve to be happy, and I know you understand this. Thank you for loving me.

My love also goes out to both my sisters, my mother, and my extended family. I wish them joy and God's blessings. As for Linda, we shall meet one day in heaven.

This book would not be complete without acknowledging one more dear soul, my best friend, my stepson, Robby. One day he enlightened me while I was very depressed and in the midst of an episode. We had been talking about my childhood, and I mentioned to him that I felt like a failure in life. His immediate response; "You're not a failure. This was not your fault, and those were not your choices in life. You didn't cause your childhood or your father to do the things he did to you. You did not do anything wrong. You were a child. It's just how you ended up. It's the family you were given."

I thought about his words long and hard. This was profound coming from a teenager. His words of wisdom inspired me to write this book also. In that instant, something in me had changed. I had still been questioning what I had done to cause the events of my childhood. Somehow, I took on that responsibility. I was playing the "what if" game. What had I messed up or what would have been different maybe if I was a better child? Robby's words changed my thinking and my outlook. A weight was lifted off me. Another sense of freedom. The removal of a burden I had carried for years. I did not do anything to cause my father to hurt me or my sisters.

Robby gave me a new perspective; my abusive childhood was not my doing. Although Robby and I live a distance from each other, we stay in touch. He is someone I can always go to for help, and it works both ways. I will always be there for him, and he will always be in my heart!

Finally, as for parents or for people entering relationships, I wanted to raise the issue of abuse in a partner. I wish my mother would have recognized these traits in my father or someone would have intervened on her behalf. This would have prevented the entire situation. Therefore, I am advocating prevention as well as intervention. After reading "12 Traits of an Abuser" by Linda Petherbridge on the Christian Broadcasting Network, I thought it very important to include this in my book. This article can be found at: https://www1.cbn.com/marriage/12-traits-of-an-abuser.

I think there are many people living in abusive situations and whose lives are miserable. The abuser is ruining joy, putting them in danger, and depriving them and their children of happiness, peace and real love. After reading Petheridge's article, I thought that this could be used as a checklist of behavior. My father met many of the characteristics such as the charm, the control, his cruelty, his criticism, and severe mood swings.

If you or someone you know is experiencing domestic violence, call the National Domestic Violence Hotline at 1-800-79-SAFE. Call the police. Call your friend or family. Scream. RUN. Do not stay. Do not take it. Do not succumb to the insanity.

**The End**